JUNGLE STORIES

THE FIGHT FOR THE
AMAZON

STING
AND
JEAN-PIERRE
DUTILLEUX

Photographs by Jean-Pierre Dutilleux

BARRIE & JENKINS
LONDON

To my children, Joe, Kate, Mickey and Jake
Sting

I dedicate this book
to my daughter Alexandra for her courage in my absence,
to my parents for their love,
and to the people of the Fourth World for having kept me alive . . .
Jean-Pierre Dutilleux

This book was first published in Great Britain in 1989 by
Barrie & Jenkins, 289 Westbourne Grove, London W11 2QA

Original French edition © Editions Jean-Claude Lattes 1989
This edition © Barrie & Jenkins Ltd 1989

Text © Sting and Jean-Pierre Dutilleux 1989
Photographs © Jean-Pierre Dutilleux

British Library Cataloguing in Publication Data
Sting
Jungle stories: the fight for the Amazon.
1. South America. Amazon River Basin
I. Title II. Dutilleux, Jean-Pierre
981'.1063

ISBN 0-09-971540-6

Typeset by SX Composing Ltd, Rayleigh, Essex
Printed in France
by Maury S.A. Malesherbes

ACKNOWLEDGMENTS
Jean-Pierre Dutilleux would like to thank
Steve Barth, Lorne and Lawrence Blair, Marlon Brando, Stewart Copeland,
Cultural Survival, Max Gail, Michel Gost, Xavier Gelin, Martin Goldsmith,
Georges Golem, Harris Foundation, Captain Kelly, Bernard Laine,
Bill Leimbach, Michael Lindsay, Bruce Marquardt, Peter Miller, Harold Ramis,
Raoni, Red Crow, Skylight, Trudie Styler, Claudio and Orlando Vilas-Boas,
and all the friends who have supported him through thick and thin over
the years.

CONTENTS

INTRODUCTION

How did I get myself into this? I found myself in the Brazilian jungle almost by accident in 1987, largely due to the efforts of one Jean-Pierre Dutilleux. The events that took place there changed my life, for to visit the forest just once is to be haunted forever after by its mysterious beauty and to be made aware of just how important its preservation is to everyone on the planet.

In this book Jean-Pierre and I try to explain what's going on in the Brazilian rain-forest, what happened to us and what hopefully can be done to stop the destruction. I hope you will enjoy the book and that it conjures for you some of the magic of the rain-forest and of the people who live there.

If we can succeed in our plan and convince as many people as possible that there is something they can do, then I will get out from under the feet of our ecologist friends and get back to singing for a living.

Sting

OCÉANO ATLÁNTICO

OCÉANO PACÍFICO

OCÉANO ATLÁNTICO

Boa Vista

Rio Negro

Japurá

Rio Branco

Manaus

Rio Amazonas

Belém

Fortaleza

Juruá

Purús

Madeira

Tapajós

Xingu

Tocantins

Recife

Rio Branco

Pôrto Velho

Bang Bang

Tocantins

São Francisco

Salvador

Guaporé

Cuiabá

Araguaia

Brasilia

Belo Horizonte

Campo Grande

São Paulo

Rio de Janeiro

Paraná

Curitiba

Uruguay

Pôrto

THE AMAZON RAINFOREST

The Amazon is the mightiest river in the world, second in length only to the Nile and first in terms of volume of water carried and the size of the area drained by it. At its mouth, which is about 168 miles wide (nearly six times the width of the English Channel at Dover), it is said to pour out more than 150,000 cu.yds of water every second.

The Amazon and its tributaries flow through a vast plain which stretches from the plateau of Guyana in the north and the Andes in the west to the Brazilian plateau in the south. The streams that feed it start near the Pacific, in the icy heights of the Andes mountains in Peru. The Xingu tributary, on the banks of which the Kapayo Indians reservation is established, flows 1230 miles from its source in the Mato Grosso to its meeting with the Amazon.

The Amazon basin has a hot, humid climate and is covered by dense tropical rainforest, one of the principal sources of oxygen for the whole planet.

In the last twenty years fabulous mineral resources have been discovered in the sub-soil. To enable them to be exploited, the Brazilian government has cut a motorway 3107 miles long, the Trans-Amazonian highway, right through the forest. Since World War II exploitation of the forest by slash-and-burn farming, logging, mining and ranching has destroyed over half the forest. Experts predict that at this rate the entire forest will have been destroyed within the next hundred years, with catastrophic consequences for the planet.

THE DYING RAINFORESTS

The Amazon is dying. Rainforests around the world are dying. The forest, the wealth of plant and animal life, indigenous peoples and their ancient cultures, the hope for finding new cures for diseases, and probably the health of our entire planet, are at risk. Every minute that goes by, 60 acres of rainforest are destroyed worldwide. Every 16 minutes, we lose an area of rainforest the size of New York's Central Park. In 1988, an area the size of Belgium was cut down and destroyed beyond all hope of recovery.

It is not alarmist to say that the Amazon could be a desert in a matter of decades. There was once a similar rainforest in North Africa. Today, we know the area as the Sahara.

We people of other nations are not remote and uninvolved witnesses. We share the blame and we must find a way to heal the rainforest.

STING
IN THE
AMAZON

After my concert in Rio de Janeiro in December 1987, Jean-Pierre Dutilleux offered to take me and my companion, the actress Trudie Styler, to visit the Amazon rainforest. The Indians Dutilleux wanted to visit were the Kayapos of the Xingu region. On the way we had to stop in Brasilia to obtain official permits for the trip . . .

BREAKFAST IN BRASILIA

BREAKFAST IS MY FAVOURITE MEAL OF THE DAY, IT always has been, there's the fresh promise of eternity in the smell of roasting coffee and as the song says, "there's an awful lot of it in Brazil". Anything seems possible today. The breakfast room of the hotel is full of well-heeled refugees from the Goiania radiation tragedy sitting out their exile in Brasilia. They were all at last night's show and thank me for dedicating one of my songs to the people of Goiania, who have become pariahs to the rest of Brazil since the x-ray leakage: no one will go there or buy any of their products because of fear of radiation.

Trudie and I sheepishly turn to our hopefully unpolluted breakfast while signing autographs for the staff and their children. We are waiting for Jean-Pierre Dutilleux (alias J.P.), a Belgian film maker of our acquaintance who has offered to take us to visit the Indians of the Xingu River. The Indians were only contacted 15 years ago and J.P. made a film about one of them, a charismatic warrior chieftain called Raoni. The film was nominated for an Oscar and Raoni became a celebrity and a spokesman for Indian rights.

J.P. arrives, smiling. He smiles almost all the time, even when there's bad news.

"We can't go," he smiles.

"Why not?"

"Because the FUNAI don't want us to."

"Who the hell are they?"

"The Bureau of Indian Affairs – they're afraid you'll shoot your mouth off about what's going on there."

"What's going on there?"

J.P., still smiling, rubs his finger and thumb together. "Corruption," he shrugs. "The conglomerates and the logging companies pay the bureau to turn a blind eye while they go into the forests to steal a hardwood tree. The real problem is that to get to that one valuable tree, they have to slash and burn a whole acre of forest. Sixty acres every minute of every day are destroyed in the Amazon basin. The only protection the forest has is the Indians – soon there will be no forest."

Trudie and I both look glum. The coffee seems to be reneging on its promise.

"Don't worry, there's still a chance. I'm going to

11

try to get Raoni on the radio. Finish your breakfast. I'll be back in an hour."

A BRUSH WITH THE AUTHORITIES

J.P. floats out of the restaurant and smiles at a large Brazilian girl struggling with a six-foot package. She erects it in the front of our table and tears off the brown paper to reveal a hideous portrait of myself looking like Boris Karloff in his most celebrated role. "It's really lovely," I lie. "Isn't it Trudie?" My companion suddenly finds the design of the sugar bowl of intense and unflinching interest. The manager of the hotel suddenly appears behind the girl. "My daughter," he explains, "thought you would like to buy it." A telephone rings in the lobby.

"Ah, that'll be the phone." I suggest. "Excuse me." Not an inspired exit but an exit nonetheless.

From the comparative safety of my room, I can see the sterile sprawl of Brasilia, a city built only in 1960 as the new capital of Brazil in an attempt to encourage the development of the country's vast empty spaces. Brasilia is in the middle of nowhere. Grey clouds hang over the city. It's going to rain again.

Trudie comes back to the room. "Thanks for leaving me."

"Well, what was I supposed to do? Be rude to the girl?"

"You weren't exactly polite."

"O.K. then, why don't we buy it and put it in the kids' room," I suggest, "and scare them to sleep at night?"

The phone rings and saves Trudie a caustic reply. "Hello?"

It's J.P. "We're back on."

"How come?"

"We managed to patch together a phone line between the president of FUNAI and Raoni's radio – and he told them to mind their own business. He wants to meet you and the Bureau of Indian Affairs can go and er . . . fuck themselves."

"You mean he's heard of me?"

"He knows you played to 200,000 people last week in Rio."

"Really – how come?"

"Er . . . I just told him. Meet me at the airport in 30 minutes."

A GLOBAL THREAT

Tropical deforestation is arguably the most dangerous threat the world has ever faced. The imminent destruction of the world's rainforests – through slash-and-burn agriculture, cattle grazing, logging, mining, dams and road building – is a crisis comparable to the threat of nuclear war. The consequences, global in scope, are potentially devastating: flooding, erosion, deserts, silting of streams and reservoirs, and climate changes worldwide.

Like nuclear war, the scope of the problem is such that people practise a kind of cognitive denial, blocking the problem out. Global warming trends and rising oceans threaten catastrophes that paralyze the mind. The average person just doesn't want to hear about it.

The issues are complex – as complex as the amazing ecosystem of the rainforest itself.

Saving the rainforest, saving the planet, saving ourselves – for we will not accomplish one without the others – requires understanding and action. We have to understand the processes at work both inside and outside the forest; social, political and economic factors in developing countries and industrialized nations alike. Moreover, we have to expand our awareness, examining our values and our priorities in how our actions affect and are affected by the world around us.

And once we understand, we have to act – immediately. Very soon it will be too late.

"Wait a minute. What shall we bring?"

"A toothbrush – bye!"

We rush to the lobby to say goodbye to Bill Francis, my tour manager. "The car's here." I look in horror at the revolting limousine they picked us up in yesterday. "I thought I told you to get rid of that monstrosity," I said. I hate limos and this one looks like it belonged to the Munsters. Bill shrugs as we grudgingly climb into the coffin-like interior that stinks of disinfectant and stale cigarette smoke.

"If the Indians don't have you for Sunday lunch, I'll see you in Porto Alegre on Tuesday. Good luck and watch out for Captain Kelly." He slams the door and waves to our grinning driver.

"What's he on about?"

"I don't know. He's just jealous that he's not going!"

All the way to the airport, cars pull alongside us honking their horns and flashing their lights at us in our funereal limousine. Hands clutching autograph books thrust from windows, flash bulbs popping from back seats. We are at the head of an hysterical convoy. Is it my imagination or can I see my portrait stuffed into the back of one of the pursuing cars?

"Let's get out of here!"

CAPTAIN KELLY

At the airport, we meet Mino Cinelu, my percussionist, who has wanted to visit the Amazon ever since he saw J.P.'s film about Raoni.

"You excited Mino?"

"Ooski," he replies.

"Where's J.P.?"

"He's loading the ooski into the ookaroo, mon capitanski!" Mino has invented a language of only

two words – all nouns are "ookaroo" and all adjectives, expletives, negatives, affirmatives are "ooski". He means that J.P. is loading supplies into the plane. I set off to find the ookaroo.

"Give me a hand," says J.P.

There's a lot of stuff to get into the six-seater airplane. "We're going to have to make two trips." I lift one very heavy package into the compartment behind the plane.

"What's in here J.P. – guns?"

J.P. smiles strangely. "No. We have to take them presents – fish hooks, torches, fishing lines, machetes, knives, aluminium pots. They have no metal. They will give us stuff in return, you'll see. Captain Kelly will bring the food on the second trip. Clive, come and meet Sting."

The forest seen from the Amazon river

I turn to face an unholy vision. Captain Kelly is over six-and-a-half feet tall in sandals, shorts and-sleeveless flak jacket; his arms, legs and chest are covered in exotic tattoos that teasingly vanish inside his clothing – a walking willow pattern. Around his neck and wrist are Indian necklaces and bangles; jungle knife strapped to a snake-skin belt; a pair of bright red spectacles that wouldn't look out of place on Elton John; a haircut that makes him look like a fugitive from Herman's Hermits – all nicely topped off with a broad Mancunian accent.

"Nice to meet you." My hand is gripped in a vice.

"Captain Kelly took me around the world," says J.P. "He knows the Xingu. He'll look after us." I flash on Billy's face as we left the hotel – Captain Kelly is straight out of the *Beano*.

To get one valuable hardwood tree, the logging companies have to slash and burn one whole acre of forest. Sixty acres every minute of every day are destroyed in the Amazon basin. The only protection the forest has is the Indians.

Once the plane is loaded, Mino and I squeeze into the back among the supplies. Trudie and J.P. face us, with the two Brazilian pilots in front – nice and cozy. We take off in a rainstorm and climb gingerly through darkening thunder clouds, a child's plaything among the elements. I prefer small planes even in turbulent weather – there's something of the mass tomb in a big jet. Somehow, airplanes that size don't feel as if they should be thrown around in the sky. In a small plane, it makes sense. I can fly upside down in one

Aerial view of the forest

and not bat an eyelid and, anyway, there's the comforting thought that in an emergency you could always make a grab for the controls. You have no such comfort on a 747.

"You O.K. Mino?"

"Ooski mon capitaine."

PIT STOP IN A MINING TOWN

We climb into the sunshine after about an hour on the roller coaster and we all want to pee. "How much further?" The pilots, by their gestures, indicate that it could be half an hour or three. Panic sweeps around the plane.

"We can land," says J.P., pointing to the east with his finger. I look out the window at a small town in the scrub. Just one street, but a blot on the landscape. We circle low over the town, the wing tips almost touching the rooftops. The pilot clearly thinks he's Nelson Piquet, Brazil's Formula One racing champion.

"Er, why are we buzzing this village?" I ask.

"So that they'll know to send a taxi for us."

"We can have a sandwich and a beer," smiles J.P. The pilot finds a reasonably flat field and lands us with a minimum of fuss. We abandon the plane as if it was about to explode, spreading to the four corners of the field to relieve the call of nature. No sooner are flies zipped than the taxi arrives, an ancient wreck with a flat tyre and a front fender dragging along the ground. Its driver looks delighted – it's hard to imagine him doing much business here. He opens the door of the cab for us, but it's already taken – in the centre of the back seat is an enormous bug of science fiction proportions.

"Going our way?" I ask. But before the bug has time to answer, our driver has clubbed him over the head and thrown him out the other door.

The bumpy ride into town makes us glad that our bladders are empty. The town itself is a squalid collection of adobe structures and wooden huts strung in a ramshackle line along the main thoroughfare. The driver passes a number of bars that look O.K., but we are clearly being driven to his brother's place at the other end of town. It's not bad, all formica and sixties furniture but the beer is cold and the sandwiches are fresh.

It's amazing how interesting a bunch of gringos drinking beer can be to people bored out of their minds. They stare at us with a macabre and unembarrassed intensity. Then a couple of honchos push to the front, wearing gold watches, bracelets, belts, buckles and guns.

"What do they want J.P.?"

"Don't worry," he says, smiling of course, inviting them to join us. We smile at the honchos. They smile at us. The spectators continue to stare. The object of the game is suddenly revealed. From his pocket one of our honchos produces a plastic bag stuffed with hundreds of emeralds.

Cultivation of coca leaves to satisfy the world's cocaine habit is blamed for the destruction of 1.7 million acres of rainforest in Peru alone.

"Ooski," gasps Mino.

I have to say the magic of precious stones is totally lost on me. Suppressing a yawn, Trudie and I exit the bar to the bewilderment of everyone there. We leave our budding Indiana Jones to haggle over the emeralds and set off for an afternoon stroll. Everywhere, there is the curious spectacle of poverty and precious metals. This is Brazil, where incredible wealth and squalid poverty are perennial bedfellows. When I see a young man clutching a dog-eared copy of *The Dream of the Blue Turtles* pointing to my face and saying "Eshtingue, Eshtingue", the Brazilian pronunciation of Sting, I realize it is time to get out of town.

I sign his record with as little fuss as possible, walk calmly back to the bar, interrupt the negotiations and head back to the airplane. I quell complaints

about the incredible deals being made by reminding everyone that we came here to visit the Indians and that time is getting on – we don't need to be looking for a jungle airfield in the dark.

XINGU, THE FORBIDDEN AREA

When we reach the airfield, our two pilots are in heated discussion. J.P. asks them what's up. The Portuguese is thick, fast and unintelligible. After about five minutes, J.P. tells us to get back into the plane.

"What was wrong?"

"Nothing.'

"J.P., was something wrong?"

"Well, it's just that the Bureau contacted the owner of the airline and told him to stop this plane getting to the Xingu."

Again J.P. makes that gesture with his finger and thumb. "Everyone has a stake in the business. The pilots have been instructed to tell us that there's something wrong with the plane and we have to turn back."

"So where are we going?"

"We are going to Xingu."

"Why?"

"Because the pilot's daughter likes you."

As the song says, "There's more to this journey than is apparent to the eye".

Now that we're out of the clouds, we can see the land below us stretching to the horizon. It's a desert of red dust. J.P. looks sad.

"All of this was rainforest ten years ago," says J.P. A few isolated stumps are left, a sad reminder of former glories. It's the sickening devastation of scorched earth, the kind of damage only men can wreak. I feel angry for my children and their children, being robbed of the earth's beauty for the sake of a few lousy bucks.

"We lose 100 species of plant and animal every day," says our guide. "Who knows, a cure for Aids or cancer could have existed down there, just waiting to

WELCOME TO THE RAINFOREST

Most of the life in the jungle lives in the canopy of trees which are up to 200 feet tall. The scaffolding of tree trunks supporting tangled branches and lianas is home to a diversity of plant and animal life unequalled on the planet. In the Amazon there are giant harpy eagles, howler monkeys, toucans, hornbills and sloths. In other rainforests there are flying squirrels, flying frogs, even flying snakes.

By contrast, the forest floor is relatively open. It is also a dark place, as it receives only five percent of the sunlight which shines on the uppermost leaves of the canopy. The jungle floor is home to plodding animals, ranging from the turkey fowl, tapir, and hosts of beetles, to the ubiquitous termites and ant-eaters. Man lives here as well.

The trees are deceptively varied. While a temperate forest in Europe or North America might have, at most, fifteen different kinds of tree, in Amazonia there are hundreds of varieties. There are 1,600 species of birds in the Amazon, more than anywhere else on earth. And two-and-a-half acres of South American forest might be home to as many as 40,000 *different species* of insects. In all, there are an estimated one million species of plant and animal in the Amazon.

be discovered, it's a living laboratory. But what do we do? We burn it wholesale. It's criminal."

The plane drones through the afternoon. "So why doesn't someone do something about it?"

"Look, Sting, this is the last frontier. You are visiting a place that very few white people have ever seen. No president of Brazil has ever visited this area. We can't depend on anyone else. Each person that comes here has to take responsibility. Look, there's the Indian border."

The sight below us is remarkable. The wasteland suddenly ends in an abrupt wall of gigantic forest. Two planets have been juxtaposed. A dead and devastated world, cheek by jowl with a world of green beauty and ebullient life.

"Where the Indians are, the forest is protected, and where they aren't, it is not. That's why the Indians are being systematically wiped out."

There used to be six million Indians in the Amazon basin. Now there are only two hundred thousand. They've been massacred, sometimes by guns, sometimes by blankets dropped on villages impregnated with flu virus, destroyed by alcohol and the demoralization of their culture.

"How big is the protected area of the Xingu?"

"It's about the size of Belgium. It's a showpiece. The tribe we're visiting are a peaceful tribe, but they are protected by the hostile tribes of the Lower Xingu of which Raoni is the chief."

"How hostile?" J.P. doesn't answer.

Through the dense forest a highway has been carved, as straight as an arrow, traversing north-south.

"The Trans-Amazonian highway. Traffic is not allowed to stop. Anyone who entered the forest would be killed by Indian patrols."

A Xingu Indian house

We all suddenly realize that we're not entering Disneyland. J.P. just smiles.

An Indian Village

Nothing can prepare you for your first glimpse of an Indian village. The symmetry of enormous thatched long-houses arranged in a perfect circle and surrounded by the chaos of the jungle. Someone flashes a mirror at us. It's a signal from another world, but as we get closer to the centre of the circle we can make out the markings of a soccer pitch and goal posts. It was the first indication that this journey was to shatter a number of fantasies we had about the Indians, as well as confirm others.

Tiny figures emerge from their houses to watch our descent to a nearby airfield. Another bumpy landing. As the door opens the jungle heat is almost solid and the silence of the late afternoon, after the twin engines have come to a stop, is wonderful and frightening. The jungle wall is as silent as a tomb.

21

Indian children

Our hosts suddenly appear at the other end of the field. Some are on bicycles, others are wearing football stripes, some are naked except for a piece of cloth around their waists.

"Why are they running towards us, J.P.?"

"They know we have presents. Hang on to your stuff. The children have got into bad habits."

As they get closer, we can make out tribal face paint, incongruous with the football stripes.

"The villages play each other. They have a league," says J.P.

They stop within six feet of us and stare.

"Blond hair is strange to them."

I suppose we're staring at them, too. All the men have a kind of Henry V haircut matted with red dye. Their faces look Tibetan, which reminds me just how far their ancestors must have travelled from the centre of Asia, north across the Bering Strait to Alaska and south through what became Canada and the United States, to Central America and finally to a southern tributary of the Amazon basin; moving about one hundred miles per generation according to studies by anthropologists.

The children are the first to touch us. They have beautiful faces. Trudie makes friends.

23

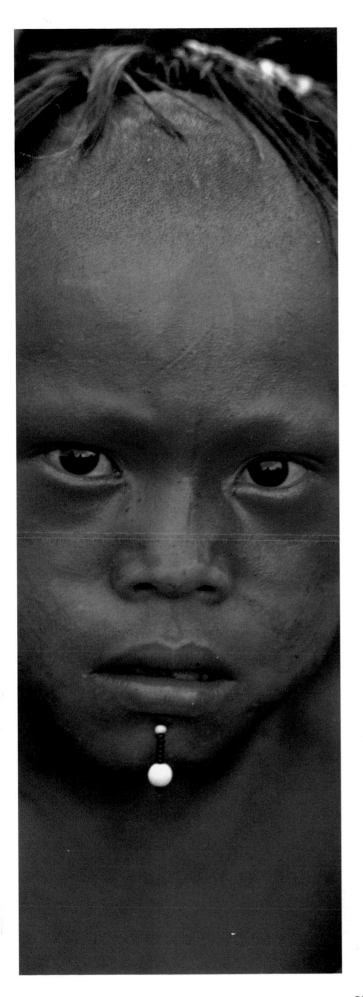

Piranha Paranoia

The airfield separates the villages from what J.P. calls the "outpost", a couple of brick houses, one belonging to a white doctor. "We'll be sleeping there." The children show us the way.

"Well, it ain't the Sheraton." A concrete floor, a rare spring bed frame, one filthy window. We decide we'd rather sleep outside, so we rig the hammocks between some trees overlooking the river. We hear our airplane take off for Brasilia.

"Where do we wash?"

"The river, of course!"

"Um, the river." I had made a promise to myself that I wouldn't go near the river because in every film I've ever seen about the Amazon, someone always gets eaten by piranhas if they even put so much as a big toe near the water.

Still, it looks really inviting when you've been travelling all day and there's no other running water.

"We lose 100 species of plant and animal every day in the Amazon. Who knows, a cure for Aids or cancer could have existed here.

Resolution out of the window, the four of us are naked and running down the river bank. The children are amused by the whiteness of our bodies and our pubic hair. Soon, I've forgotten the piranha and I'm adding my own stream to the river's flow, when I suddenly remember what a friend of mine told me about the Amazon, – never pee in the river because the urine attracts a tiny fish that screws itself into your penis and stays there. I hurriedly stop myself and remove myself from the danger zone.

"Mino, you peeing?"

"Ooski."

"Er, I think we should get out now."

J.P. taps me on the shoulder and, speaking with a reverential quiet, says, "Raoni is here."

27

RAONI, GREAT INDIAN CHIEF

Above, on the river bank, is a tall man with shoulder length hair, ceremonial beads and Levis. Between his chin and his bottom lip is a large wooden plate. He has the good sense to be peeing into the river from a great height, while waving to us with his free hand. He is an impressive figure, the chief of the Kayapo, a great and famous warrior. We scramble into our clothes for an audience with the great man.

J.P. and Raoni greet each other with great ceremony and the true affection of those who have shared many adventures. Raoni looks at all of us with a friendly intensity, weighing our personalities, while we stare back and try not to let our eyes stray to the plate around which his lower lip is painfully stretched. Raoni and J.P. converse in a basic Portuguese. He points to Mino's earring and asks J.P. if he is a woman. He tells J.P. that I am very pretty and that Trudie is braver than both of us put together.

Above: Indian warriors
Left: Raoni, chief of the Kayapo Indians

THE WORLD'S OLDEST ECOLOGICAL SYSTEM

Rainforests are the earth's oldest ecological system. Over the millions of years these forests have been standing, evolution has created an organism to fill every niche.

As lush as they are, though, tropical forests grow on soils which are poor in nutrients. The forest must maintain its own food chain, forming an efficient, closed system by storing its nutrients above ground in the living vegetation. Nutrients enter the chain in rainfall, but once they are part of the forest, they remain. Leaves and other dead matter (plant and animal) which fall to the forest floor are broken down by bacteria and fungi incredibly fast, reducing the debris to raw, organic elements to be immediately reabsorbed by the living plants. Under the intense tropical sun, the rainforest maintains its own environment by blocking out the sun and wind, locking in the heat and humidity.

Rainforests are also called "closed forests" because they maintain their own humidity through a process called transpiration, by which plants take in carbon dioxide and release oxygen and moisture, in much the same way as we release carbon dioxide and moisture when we exhale. More than half the rain that falls in some rainforests precipitates from moisture produced by the jungle itself.

The food chain in the rainforest is very complex and also very fragile. When the forest is cut and burned for farming, the initial richness of the soil is short-lived and can only support crops for a few years. Then the farmer has no choice but to move on to another patch of virgin forest.

The fact that trees remove carbon from the air is very important. Not only does the burning of the forests limit the green world's ability to scrub the air, but the burning itself sends massive amounts of pollution into the atmosphere.

"Raoni likes to joke," explains J.P.

"He wants to take you to the village of Aritana, the chief of the Iaualapitis. It's the village we flew over, the one that signalled us. Let's go before it gets dark."

We set off on foot behind Raoni. He is flanked by two warriors who keep turning around to give us the death stare.

"Why are they looking at us like that, J.P.?"

"Probably because the last time they saw a white man, they killed him."

"Oh."

Raoni reminds me of someone, but I can't think who it is. He walks through the forest as if he owns it. As we approach the village, we begin to hear periodic whoops and yelps. Some kind of ceremony is taking place. I try to cast Billy's image of the cooking pot from my mind.

We enter the circle of houses like fugitives from an episode of *Star Trek* gazing in wonder at an alien world. The circle is deserted, but the noise of the ceremony is coming from a house to our right.

My picture of an Indian village before this visit would not have included the word "grandeur", but "grandeur" is just the right word to describe the scale and dignity of their architecture. It neither dwarfs the forest nor is dominated by it, it is intrinsically part of the forest. There is no clutter, no squalor or poverty, but a "rightness", a balance with nature in such contrast to the degrading chaos of Rio and to the ugliness of the mining town we have just left.

Another tribal whoop breaks the silence and Chief Aritana emerges from a doorway in head-dress, face and body paint, parrot feathers attached to his arms, followed by about twenty similarly clad warriors. He greets J.P. and tells him that he can't stay and chat because he has to perform a ceremony in every house to chase away evil spirits.

The men head for the next house in a workman-like posse, like men setting out to fix a roof. It makes perfect sense. The women and children follow. There is a prevalent sense of fun that doesn't contradict the

THE WORLD'S RAINFORESTS

There are about five million remaining square miles of tropical rainforest, found around the world, between the Tropic of Capricorn and the Tropic of Cancer, where there is more light, heat and moisture than anywhere else on the planet. Since the end of World War II, wholesale exploitation has destroyed nearly half the original rainforest. Scientists estimate that, at present rates of exploitation, the forests will be gone, completely and forever, sometime within the next 100 years.

The largest concentrations of jungle are in three areas. In Asia, the jungle extends from Burma through Malaysia, Indonesia and New Guinea to Queensland, Australia. In West Africa, the rainforest is mostly in Zaire. And in Latin America, the jungle runs from the Yucatan Penninsula to Bolivia, and includes the Amazon, the world's largest single rainforest.

Amazonia is nearly as big as the continental United States and encompasses the largest river system in the world, the Amazon River and its tributaries. The majority of the Amazon region is in Brazil, covering 3 million square miles. The Amazon accounts for about half the world's remaining tropical forest.

solemnity of the occasion. Raoni looks on with great satisfaction and lights a Xingu cigarette. This is the keystone of Raoni's cause – the preservation of a culture of which Aritana's village may be one of the last unadulterated examples.

MUSIC AND GUNS

After half-an-hour, the sun has set and the ceremony is over. A new event is on the timetable. Some of the women spirit Trudie away to one of the houses, for no woman is allowed to see this ritual. Three large flutes are taken from the central hut which is a kind of village parliament and we witness a primordial musical event, lit by the moon and of such hypnotic intensity that we all feel drugged and deliciously far from home, but it touches something in each of us that we recognize as ours. This is our home too, under the moon and the stars, with the din of the forest and the drone of the flutes. The city makes no sense at all.

I glimpse Raoni moving to the rhythm of the music with his feet and, in that one gesture, I realize who it is that he reminds me of. The intrinsic dignity, kingliness and power that was Bob Marley, a man I met only once but would never forget. Here is his forest counterpart – the King of the Amazon, a champion of the oppressed, the voice of a nation. I notice Mino discreetly taping the performance on his Walkman, cautious of taboo, respectful, but desperate to retain something of this moment. J.P. looks positively beatific.

The performance is over and Trudie is brought into the open. "How was it?"

"I can't tell you how it was. They made me lie in a hammock by a fire in the darkness, all of the women were quite still and we could hear the noise of the flutes. I felt as if I was back in the womb, in the belly of a dark ship." She looks at me strangely. "Like being at home."

Megaron, the cousin of Aritana, catches my eye and talks to J.P. while still looking at me.

"He wants to know why you're sad."

"I'm not sad."

"He says you are."

"I'm not." I pretend that I've seen something in the forest and look away.

We walk back in the darkness to the outpost where they're preparing some food for us. Manioc bread, fish, rice and beans, gelatinous coffee by candlelight, flanked by warriors and staring children. The food is delicious.

"I made a joke today, J.P., and you smiled, but you didn't laugh."

"Really?"

"Yes, I asked if one of the cases had guns in it." J.P. smiles stiffly. "Well, did it have guns in it?"

"No!"

"Then why are you reacting so strangely?"

"It's a long story."

"We have all night."

The candle flickers in the dark room. All eyes are on J.P.

"Well, eleven years ago, when I made the film about Raoni, I gave the Indians half the royalties. I got them a bank account in Sao Paulo. It was at a time when a lot of Indians had been massacred by white men with guns.

"I met Raoni in Sao Paulo and he said he needed my help. I said, 'Anything. What is it?' He told me he'd emptied the bank account in Sao Paulo and bought 100 rifles and ammunition. I was shocked, but Raoni said it was the only way the Indians would survive, by defending themselves. He wanted me to get the guns to the Amazon for him. I said no, that I could go to prison for gun running. He told me that if I was truly a friend of the Indians, I would have to comply with his wishes. I had to agree, although I was terrified. Raoni reassured me that they were just for hunting. I managed to get a plane and we set off for the jungle with the guns. Everything went smoothly until we ran out of fuel and had to land at an air force base and we spent the night in sleeping bags around the plane in case anyone got curious."

The candle is guttering in the evening breeze. As much as I hate guns, I realize that I am in the centre of a war – a war where you're forced to take sides. J.P. has chosen his side and the more I learn about these people and the destruction of their rainforest, the more inclined I am to take their side. It seems to me that their culture is a true civilization. If they are destroyed, then we'll all fall like a pack of dominoes.

THE AMAZON RAINFOREST AS A RESOURCE

One quarter of our prescription drugs are derived from plants found in the rainforest, 1,400 have been found to have cancer fighting properties. Alkaloids from the leaves of the rosy periwinkle have been successful in treating Hodgkin's disease and childhood leukaemia. The bark of the Cinchona, from which quinine is made, relieves the symptoms of malaria. From the venom of the Brazilian pit viper, one of the world's deadliest snakes, comes a drug for high blood pressure. Other plant and animal compounds are the basis of treatments for schizophrenia and dysentery, and are contained in anaesthetics, muscle relaxants, antihistamines and contraceptives. Western countries import tens of thousands of tons of plant material each year for drug production. It is estimated that there may be as many unclassified plants in Amazonia as there are known varieties in all of North America.

The world's rainforests may also help to regulate the earth's weather. Rainforest vegetation absorbs water and releases it slowly. When this vital watershed is lost, catastrophic flooding can result. Deforestation in India and Nepal has already destroyed the upland watershed that protected Bangladesh's Ganges Delta from flooding in the monsoon season, affecting millions of people living there.

A NIGHT BY THE RIVER

Time for bed. We find our hammocks by torchlight. I hate mosquito nets almost as much as I hate mosquitoes. There is something macabre and shroud-like about the net. I also hate net curtains. We share our bivouac with some of Raoni's warriors, who spend the night farting and laughing. Mino and I join the conversation, much to Trudie's disgust.

"Goodnight, Trudie."

"Goodnight, Sting."

"Goodnight, Mino. Ooski."

The night song of the jungle lulls us to sleep.

I dream I am trapped in a dark house full of suffocating net curtains that I can't get through. I land with a thud, wrestling my mosquito net, the hammock swinging above me.

"Good morning, Sting."

"Er, good morning, Trudie." I hear tittering in the bushes and then a scampering towards the river. All the Indians in the outpost are heading towards the river with their toothbrushes. It is a strange sight, reminiscent of the Flintstones.

"Were you dreaming?" asks Trudie.

"I think so."

"So was I. I was dreaming about snakes."

Snakes have been a lifetime obsession for Trudie. I had seen her run screaming from a room if a snake so much as wriggled across a television screen, or come close to fainting if she happened across one of the "slimy bastards" in a David Attenborough book. The girl is utterly fearless in any kind of physical pursuit, but snakes could trigger a paranoia that was frightening in itself to behold.

Was it just fate that Trudie was offered a movie this year with only two characters? You guessed it, a girl and a snake, a black mamba to be precise. The director must have sensed something real and compelling in Trudie when they discussed the snake, even though my actress friend had no intention of agreeing to do the movie. The director became adamant that Trudie was the only person he wanted to play the role. Trudie became more and more paranoid; one, about

the snake and two, about turning down the movie. The Faustian bargain had never seemed so clear.

Cast in the role of supporting devil, I pointed out that she had no business calling herself an actress if she was going to turn down the role that others would die for (wrong metaphor?) just because she was afraid of a little snake. Well, Trudie's hackles rose and before you could say "Mephistopheles", she was on the film set with said black mamba. With an Italian film crew looking on, their curiosity reminiscent of a blood-thirsty mob from the coliseum of ancient Rome. Upon meeting her co-star, Trudie threw up on the director and jumped on the back of the cameraman, digging her nails deep into his neck and drawing blood. His wife needed more than a cursory explanation.

Above: Mino in his hammock on the banks
of the river
Left: Aerial view of an Indian village

35

Anyway, as day followed day, Trudie became less and less afraid of the snake and even grew to like it, just as her character would at first fear the creature and would then grow to dominate it. It was as if Trudie has been rehearsing her whole life for this one role. The director was pleased. Trudie felt as if she'd woken from a nightmare and I just loved the ironic symmetry, thinking that this was the satisfying last act of a psychological drama, the final resolution of "Trudie and the Snake". But I was wrong.

"Were you dreaming about your mamba again?"

"No, this was a red snake and you were wearing it."

"Me?"

"Yes, then you woke me up."

THE WITCH DOCTOR STRUCK BY LIGHTNING

J.P. had spent the night in the brick cell, ever smiling. "Have a nice night?"

"Ça va bien, mon ami. Et toi?"

"I want to take you to visit Tacuma this morning. He's an old friend of mine, the Chief of the Kamaiura and the most powerful witch doctor in the area. Three days ago, he was struck by lightning. His "number one spirit" protected him from death, but he's very weak. His village is about two hours away by bicycle. Let's get some coffee and set off."

I had not imagined this scenario – the four of us on bicycles, acting as if the Amazon jungle were Hyde Park, laughing and singing. The chain on Trudie's bike is too loose and disengages itself from the wheel. I put the chain back on, but no sooner had we gone a few yards than it comes off again. We hide the bicycle in the jungle and Trudie rides pillion while I struggle with mud. The sky looks gloomy, but we are all happy.

"Tacuma's village is by a lagoon," says J.P. "The Indians believe that all life started there. It's a large claim, but I suppose being isolated in the jungle can make one's myths a little egocentric. Anyway, life beginning in a lagoon isn't far from what modern

SLASH AND BURN AGRICULTURE

The Indians have practised slash-and-burn agriculture in the Amazon for thousands of years. Understanding the fragility of their environment, they did it on such a small scale that when they moved on to more fertile soil, the patches left fallow were small enough to grow back and rejuvenate the jungle.

On the other hand, this method of clearing the jungle for planting is being carried out on a devastating scale in the tropics today. Slash-and-burn farming, mostly by poor peasants, is the leading cause of rainforest destruction in Brazil. About 8 million hectares of rainforest are cleared this way every year.

Overpopulation is frequently cited as the main reason for agricultural homesteading in Third World rainforests. But it often has more to do with unequal distribution of the valuable farmlands – a very small percentage of the population controlling a very large percentage of the land. Without including the Amazon region, Brazil actually has about the same population density as the United States. Frequently with the co-peration of national governments and international organizations such as the World Bank, the poor are bought out or forced off their productive land and driven into the forest with unfulfilled promises of land.

After a few years of slash-and-burn farming, torrential jungle rains have leached all the nutrients from the soil, robbing the land of its ability to support crops. Then the farmer has to move on to raze another stand of forest and the land is taken over by the ranchers.

science tells us, and if I were looking for the garden of Eden, I would think that I had already found it here."

"So where's the forbidden fruit, J.P.?"

"Progress, my friend, progress."

"And the serpent?" asks Trudie.

"I believe the serpent has been much maligned in popular mythology. Originally it symbolized the feminine principle and to the Indians the snake is their most powerful symbol of strength." Everyone is suddenly silent and lost in their own thoughts, as people on journeys often are, when suddenly about 200 yards in front of us, I see something startling. It is large and black and looking down the trail at us, and then it is gone, vanishing into the forest like a ghost.

"Did you see it?" asks J.P., excited.

I gulp and answer, "Yes, I did."

"It's the panther. I heard them talking about it last night at the outpost. They have been hunting it for weeks."

There is a lot of confusion as to whether a black cat crossing your path is lucky or unlucky. My only thought was that if the cat happens to be a black panther, then we're either in for an awful lot of good luck, or an awful lot of bad luck. "Ooski." Again, we are all lost in thought when we see the lagoon before us. J.P. breaks the silence.

"There is another legend about the lagoon. They say that at dawn you can see the ghost of a white man on a horse galloping along the far shore. He is said to wear full armour, that shines in the morning sun. Maybe it's a memory of one of the Conquistadors. They were crazy people, they just set off into the jungle on some vague inexplicable quest for glory."

"Sounds like rock and roll." I feel an instant rapport with the crazy fool, doomed forever to gallop across the stage in full armour, an eternity away from home.

"You know the first white man that Raoni ever saw was a man on a horse. Raoni was a young warrior and each warrior must leave the village for a time and become a 'dream wanderer'. They go off to 'find themselves' like aboriginals on walk about." Again, I sense an echo in my own heart. I have wandered the earth for 15 years trying to find myself – a nomad with a Samsonite.

"Raoni saw this white man on a horse and he thought he had seen a demon. He ran through the forest and the white man chased him. Raoni escaped, but now he wonders if it wasn't a demon that chased him after all." We are four demons on bicycles.

Tacuma's village is identical to Aritana's. The same majestic long houses, the perfect circle, the village parliament in the centre. The children play in the security of the village, for no wild animal will enter the empty circle. They look so happy, dancing and playing. I think of the half million street kids of Sao Paulo, homeless, abandoned by their families, doomed to a life of glue sniffing and petty crimes. Six-year-olds with revolvers, sexually abused, unwanted, hardened to a world that is unthinkably cruel.

Trudie and I visited a home in Sao Paulo called Casa Serena, run by a religious brother called James, a follower of Mother Theresa. There were 60 boys in the home, aged from six to sixteen, all from the street. They ask children if they want a bed instead of the pavement. They come and go as they please and with the atmosphere of the home, they soon become children again. It was hard not to cry when these hardened criminals and glue addicts came and hugged us. They are desperate for love and affection, their hardness only a mask with which to protect themselves. These were the lucky ones; their brothers on the street will grow up hard. But back in paradise, the young are the treasure of the community, the hope for the future, the bloodline of their culture. A society that abandons its children cannot survive.

There will be Great Suffering and Anger

J.P. leads me to Tacuma's house. Inside it is like a vast dark cathedral. I am led through a series of curtains to Tacuma's chamber. A fire burns on the floor. Tacuma

Jungleburgers

In the last ten years, cattle ranching has grown to occupy 72 percent of the cleared areas of the rainforest. The beef is largely to supply hamburger meat to fast-food chains in the United States. When the ranchers need more land, they have been known to use violence to force farmers to sell their land. By the time the cattle have finished with the land, nothing is left but dust. The most productive biological system in the world becomes the most barren.

The Logging Industry

Commercial logging is the second largest cause of tropical deforestation. Much of it is taken simply for firewood or charcoal, because taking it from virgin rainforest is cheaper than harvesting secondary growth forests.

Providing tropical hardwood for construction in developed countries is another market for Amazon timber. Japan imports about half the world's annual harvest of tropical timber. Western Europe is second. America alone consumes $2 billion worth of tropical timber products every year. The use of tropical woods in paper products has increased dramatically in the last 40 years, also.

If practised properly, logging in the rainforests could be a sustainable industry. But even where there are government regulations, they are rarely heeded. Only one tree in twenty may be taken for construction timber, for instance, but up to a dozen others may be destroyed in the process. And as much as one third of the trees are removed just to make way for logging roads and tracks. More importantly, logging often opens previously untouched areas of rainforest to homesteaders, who have squatter's rights to any unclaimed land in Brazil.

Last year, in cooperation with the Rainforest Alliance, the American Institute of Architects (AIA) agreed to investigate how their profession had an effect on rainforest destruction. By unanimous vote, the AIA resolved to find alternate choices in the timber they specify for construction.

is in a hammock, two warriors tend the fire. It is estimated that Tacuma is in his seventies, although his body is that of a young man. His face is lined with the marks of great wisdom, with his eyes he can know a person in one glance.

J.P. takes his hand and kisses it like a supplicant greeting the Pope. The strangeness of the scene had something of *Apocalypse Now* about it, when Martin Sheen meets Marlon Brando. A cinematic echo of Joseph Conrad's *Heart of Darkness*. We are paying homage to our primeval history. We have stepped back in time to the Stone Age. This fire lighting the darkness has burned for a million years. I take a seat by the fire, staring into the flames. J.P. and Tacuma talk quietly. The warriors are his sons. On learning

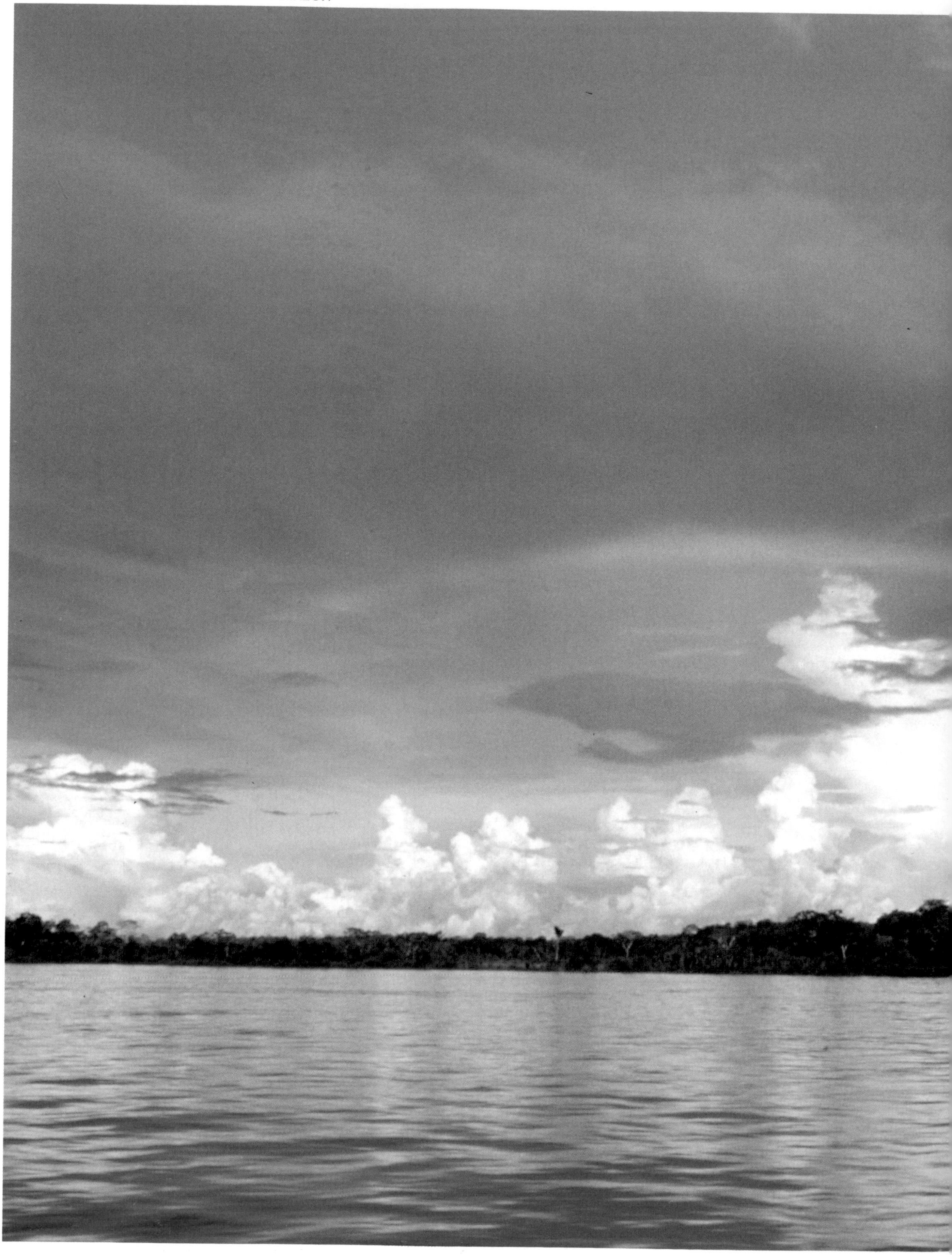

THE MINING MENACE

Mining wreaks environmental and social havoc in the Amazon. Brazil has the richest deposits of iron ore on the planet. Unfortunately, those deposits are in eastern Amazonia. Pig iron smelting furnaces require charcoal. By law, the charcoal is supposed to come only from reforested land but there is little enforcement, so about 90 percent is taken from irreplaceable primary forest instead. In one area alone seven production plants scheduled for completion by 1992 would consume 700,000 tons of charcoal per year.

More importantly, an estimated half million people are scouring the Amazon for gold. They have made Brazil the world's fifth largest gold producer. In 1988, mining companies and freelance prospectors took about 83 tons of gold from the jungle. Now entering its second decade, Brazil's gold rush is accelerating, fuelled by recession and unemployment. New claims have reached to neighbouring Venezuela, Guyana, Colombia and Bolivia.

All told, about 5 million people are involved in the economy of the gold rush. And the miners have brought much of the worst of civilization with them.

Despite laws prohibiting it, mercury is used to extract gold from river mud, resulting in mercury poisoning in downstream communities. Gold mining in the Amazon was also responsible for 12 percent of the mercury released into the atmosphere in 1988.

A pot of gold at the end of the rainbow?

THE COCAINE BUSINESS

It is worth noting, too, that another threat to the Amazon rainforest comes from the increasing cultivation of coca, the leaves of which are used to make cocaine. For instance, according to a report released by the U.S. State Department, coca cultivation and related activity is blamed for the destruction of 1.7 million acres of Peruvian rainforest, about one tenth of the total deforestation in that country since the turn of the century.

Coca has always been harvested by Indians in the Andean highlands of South America, who chew the leaves as a mild stimulant. Now however, coca has become a cash crop. As cocaine use increases and profits to be made from the leaves skyrocket, farmers are razing virgin forest to plant coca. With support from the U.S., Latin American governments are working to eradicate the crops with herbicides, but either way, forest is destroyed. The United States and Europe are the major consumers of cocaine, of course, and only a drop in market demand will discourage coca cultivation.

that, I am overtaken by a wave of sadness. I miss my father, who had died, but a week before, of cancer. When I visited him in the hospital, I thought they had sent me to the wrong bed – the disease had so eaten away at my father that I could no longer recognize him.

I remember taking his hand just as J.P. had taken Tacuma's. I searched for something to say. I told him that we had the same hands. He agreed, but said that

Preparing a meal of grasshoppers

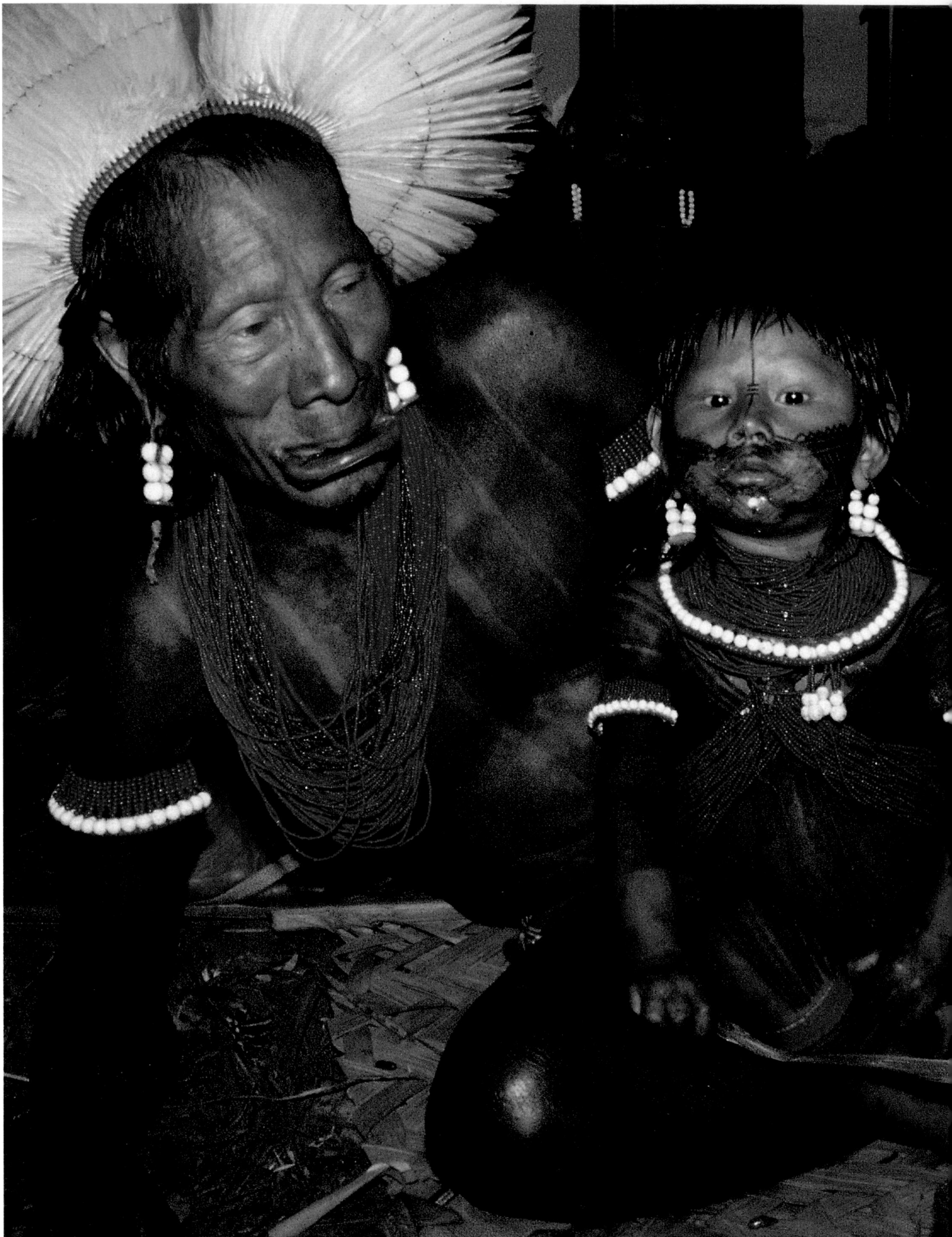

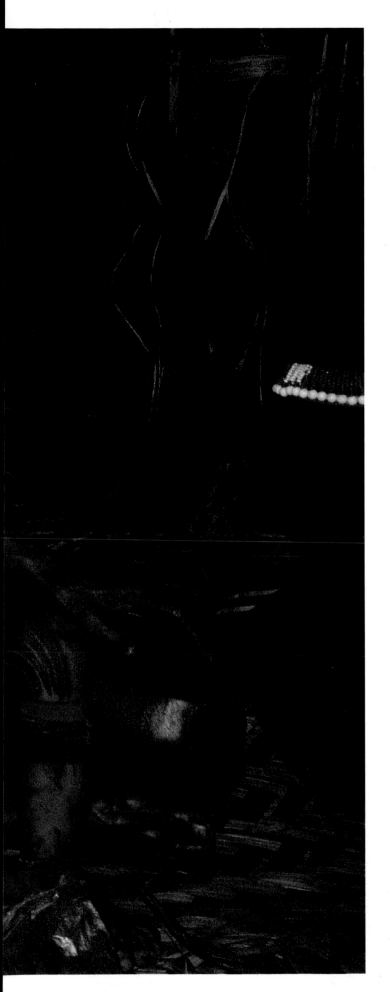

I'd put my hands to much better use than he had. He'd never paid me a compliment before, and now he was gone, except that on stage at the Marcana, I felt he was with me. In front of 200,000 people he was with me – my success was, after all, his success. Morbid are those who prefer a funeral to a wake, and here was a wake to end all wakes. Joy and sadness in equal measure.

Tacuma says he is weak from the lightning bolt. He suspects bad medicine and won't be attending the meeting this afternoon. He looks to the flames. A roar of thunder is heard outside and then the hiss of rain. Perhaps it's easy for witch doctors to have their words punctuated by the elements. A sense of drama or an acute timing, who knows, but Tacuma begins to speak with a quiet intensity. J.P. translates for me. "The rainforest is being destroyed and so are the Indians. There will be great suffering, bloodshed, pestilence,

DESTRUCTION BY FLOODING

About 125 hydroelectric dams are to be built in Brazil by the year 2010. In 1986, the World Bank approved $500 million in loans to Brazil for new hydroelectric projects. The Environmental Defense Fund warns that the proposed dams could result in the flooding of more than 60,000 acres of rainforest in the Amazon Basin, displacing as many as half a million people.

Previous World Bank loans for hydroelectric projects stipulated protection of the Indians and their environment, but that responsibilty was entrusted to FUNAI. Environmentalists accuse the Brazilian agency of neglecting its responsibility and the World Bank of failing to enforce the loans' environmental promises. Now the World Bank, citing the government's failure to protect the forest and the Indians, have held back on new loans or even disbursing funds on existing loans.

45

anger and shame." The flames of the fire begin to rise, scorching my face – the thunder roars again. "The world is in great danger, when the trees die, the earth dies. We will be orphans without a home, lost in the chaos of the storm." It feels as if Tacuma's house is afloat on a wild sea. The wind howls high above us in the rafters of the roof. We are in the hold of Noah's Ark and the rain keeps falling.

Tacuma has finished speaking. He seeks solace in the flames. J.P. and I leave quietly and walk out into the rain. I feel deeply tired as if I've been on a long journey, my eyes squinting in the daylight. We find Mino and Trudie sheltering in the central hut. We must look very strange, but I have no words to explain my feelings. The hissing of the rain speaks for us.

Plane in Distress

Between the peals of thunder, we can hear the drone of a twin-engined plane hidden by the low cloud. "That'll be Captain Kelly looking for the airfield," explains J.P. "It sounds like he's in trouble." We gaze at the darkening clouds anxiously, with only the sound of the struggling engines to guide us, and then only silence.

"He'll be O.K." I notice that J.P. has his fingers crossed. We sit out the storm. The village children find Mino endlessly amusing. He sings, laughs, does his ape act. Trudie finds a baby to cuddle. She misses the kids, so do I. The rain seems endless. I prop myself against the wall of the shelter and fall asleep. I dream of tidal waves and old wooden ships. Captain Kelly is an albatross and Trudie has wound herself around the branch of tree.

I awake to the sound of a broad Mancunian accent. "That was the worst flight of my life – bloody terrifying. But I'm here now with a plane full of goodies." The Captain is drenched to the skin, his hair is matted on one side of his head, making him look like a wet spaniel. The rain has stopped. "This might be our only chance to get back to the outpost – c'mon."

The jungle trail is too sodden even to attempt getting on the bikes and before long we are covered in mud.

"You were in Police, weren't you, Sting?" asks Captain Kelly.

"I was, yes."

"Weren't Andy Summers in the band?"

"Yeah, he was, why?"

"Oh I used to book bands in the sixties and he were in Zoot Money's Big Roll Band. I had a string of rhythm and blues clubs in the north of England and I remember Andy."

"What happened?" I asked.

'Oh, I sold them, came to Brazil and opened a big pub in Sao Paulo. It were very successful but I got the wanderlust and when the Xingu were discovered I found myself up here helping with the film making. That's how I met J.P., the crazy bastard." J.P. smiles. "You see this lad here?" He grabs one of the warriors. "He were only a little boy when I first came here, now he's a big man. He's called Megaron. I named my own son after him."

"Are you still with the same lady?" asks Trudie. An ocean of sadness seems to well up in the Captain's eyes. God, it's hard to keep your emotions in check in this place.

"No, that were a long time ago." He falls silent. The forest leaves are dripping with rain. No one feels like speaking until the Captain says, "Well then I built myself a boat and sailed around the world like the Flying Dutchman. I'm a dream wanderer too, you know." About 200 yards ahead of us is a red conflagration in one of the trees by the side of the trail. As we get closer, we see that it is a beautiful parrot, wild-eyed and staring at us.

TRADE IN THE VILLAGE

We are back in Aritana's village, in front of the parliament house, and all the fishing lines, hooks, machetes, knives are laid out on the ground. The men of the village inspect the goods like buyers at a garage

sale. Having satisfied themselves of the quality of the goods on display, they hurry back into their houses for something to trade. A head-dress, ceremonial feathers, a clay pot, a necklace of exquisite shells, a bow and arrow, the arrowheads made from the back bone of a piranha.

Trudie has brought something personal to trade (lipstick, eye shadow, lip gloss); the warriors look puzzled, so Trudie demonstrates. The phallic nature of lipstick has never been clearer. I anxiously look for a reaction from the tribesmen, thinking "One erection and we're finished." Again, they hurry back to their long-houses to show their wives. There is an erotic electricity in the air and Trudie looks very pleased with herself as she is showered with bracelets and beautiful necklaces.

On a single day in 1988, scientists recorded 6000 man-made fires burning in the Amazon rainforest. The consequences, to the forest and to the world, are devastating.

Aritana asks me to try the bow and arrow. He demonstrates with incredible grace and strength, drawing the bowstring back to this right shoulder. The bow looks as if it is about to snap and then the arrow is heading skyward, describing a perfect arc and landing in the ground halfway between the parliament and the long-houses. Now it is my turn and the whole village is watching. I haven't shot a bow and arrow since I was a kid.

"Don't fuck it up, don't fuck it up! Just breathe deeply, pull back the bow string, relax, now breathe out, but what if I hit somebody? Oh God, what if I kill a child or even a dog? Just relax, breathe again. Imagine the arrow sailing through the air. Breathe out, think of Crecy and let go." Thank God, it's not perfect, but honour is satisfied. The arrow lands behind Aritana's house. Now it's Mino's turn and, before he shoots, one of the elders who is clearly the

village wag indicates that the arrow should be aimed straight above the head. Everybody laughs and Mino declines the advice, realizing that when it comes down he'll be the target. A sense of humour in the jungle is as important as mosquito spray.

DANCE OF THE RIVER SPIRIT

By now all the chiefs of the surviving tribes have gathered for the meeting: the Kuikurus, the Kalapalos, Meinacos, Matipu, Txicaos, Txuccarramae, Suyas, Jurunas, Kajabis, Wauras. We sit among them. Raoni is aware of our discomfort. He calms us with a touch of his hand, we are in no danger. A dance begins. Four feathered warriors accompanied by a musician beating a hollow log and two boy children with twigs tied to their arms. They perform the dance of the river spirit. Occasionally, the boys make mistakes in the steps. Their fathers redirect them by yanking their arms. It is comic and yet serious. The children are assimilated into the spiritual and cultural life of the village, while our children are banished to the ghetto of the video arcade.

Their performance is over and Aritana is talking very seriously to J.P. "They want you to sing. They performed for you, now it's your turn."

"Fair enough." I look at my audience. I feel like Barry Manilow at the P.L.O.'s annual dinner dance. "Stiff upper lip, you've faced audiences as hostile as this. The ex-servicemen's club in Sunderland, the British Legion Social Club in West Hartlepool." My stiff upper lip wilts in the face of a row of stiff lower lips. Hands massaging spears and rifle butts. "You ready Mino?" "Ooski."

Sting and Mino perform for the Indians

53

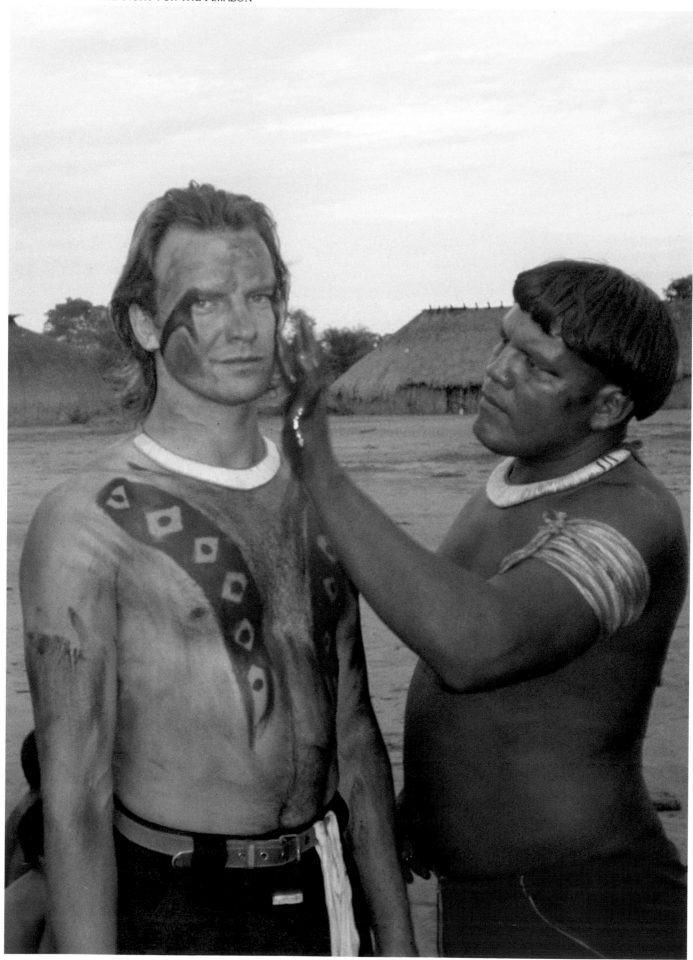

We seek out some old pots and pans from Arita-na's house and now we're facing our debut audience in the Amazon. "What shall we do, mon capitaine?" whispers Mino from the side of his mouth.

"We'll do 'Fragile – keep smiling."

A deep breath. I sing the song in Portuguese. It's about the fragility of the human frame. "Blood will flow when flesh and steel are one." I hope they like

this. Trigger fingers fidgeting. My voice wavers a little on the high notes. Mino misses a beat. "Don't panic! This is working." Second verse, much better. "Hit those notes, they can only kill you, go out singing." The song is over. One of the women giggles. I make my most theatrical bow and pause expectantly with my nose three inches from the ground. Do I hear appreciative noises? "Ooski!" whispers Mino. We both look up, they're smiling, thank God.

"They liked you," confirms J.P. I see my friend from yesterday, the one who insisted I was sad. I look at him. "J.P., ask him if I still look sad."

"He says you do."

"Tell him he's right. I'm sad because my father died and I miss him."

"He wants to know if your father was a great chief."

"Tell him my father was a chief milkman." My friend looks puzzled.

Captain Kelly is giving the children some of the biscuits that he brought. He hands me one. They are circular. By biting one of the edges, it is possible to place it in my bottom lip. "Oh–oh, Raoni has seen me. I'm dead." I walk over to him thinking I'll brazen it out, the biscuit insolently protuding from my bottom lip. Raoni bursts out laughing and then offers to make a hole in my lip with a sharp stick.

"Tell him I have a photo session next week, J.P."

Raoni grunts, satisfied that his first impression of me was correct.

"Aritana wants to paint you and Mino."

They want to paint the snake god on our chests and backs – it's their most powerful symbol. With red dye, they dab on the markings of the Surucucu Jaca do Pico, which I am told is the most deadly snake in South America. In English, he's known as the pit viper. The Surucucu Jaca do Pico is rarely seen, but like all deadly things here he is respected.

"Forty-five minutes of excruciating agony before death. Its venom attacks the central nervous system. If you get serum quickly enough you may only be paralyzed," says Trudie cheerfully, who is now of

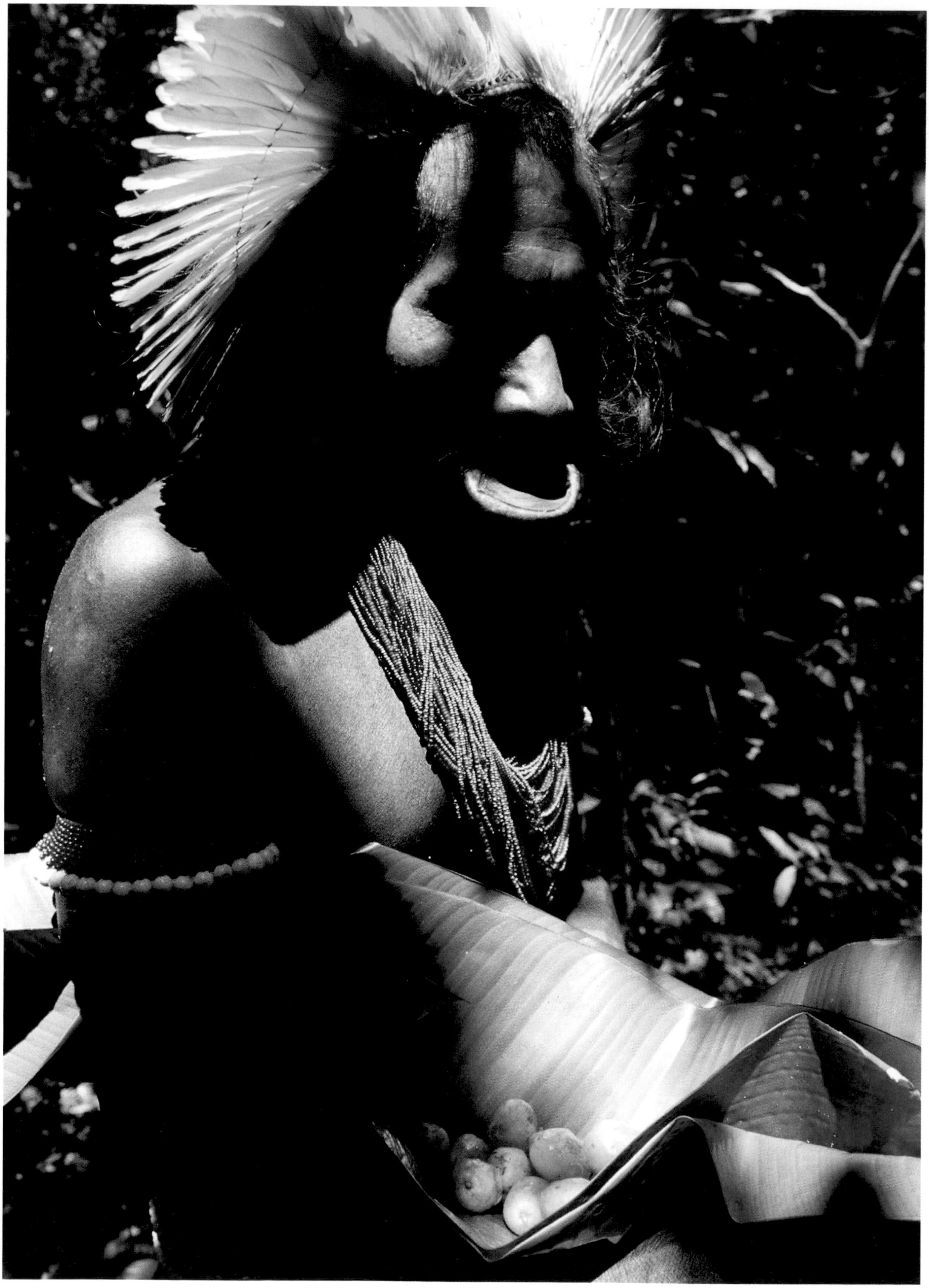

course our herpetology expert. I have charcoal and red dye all over my body.

"What do you think, Trudie?"

"Hmmm!" She gives me one of her strange looks. "You look like a bloody firework." She has two discreet arrowheads painted on her cheeks but Mino and I are in full make-up.

"Yes, I feel much more ferocious now. I've only been here 24 hours and I'm 'Lord of the Flies'. Gone are the trappings of civilization. Where's my bow and arrow?"

J.P. interrupts my reverie. "Raoni wants to talk to you seriously." We are sitting in a circle, Raoni speaks slowly and clearly despite the plate in his lip. He speaks with passion. "We want nothing from the white man. He has brought us only death, illness and murder. He has stolen and destroyed our forest. He wants to destroy it all. We want to be left alone to live as our ancestors. We want our children to inherit the forest. We Indians do not want blood mixed with that of the whites, we don't want to live in your cities. We want to stay here, it is our right. Now you must tell us what you think."

> "We Indians want nothing from the white man. He has brought us only death, illness and murder. He has stolen and destroyed our forest."

"I am honoured to be your guest here and you have treated me kindly. I believe that the forest is yours, but the white man has no real home. He is lost in a world that he doesn't understand. He has ceased to communicate with the spirits of the earth and the forest, the river and air, so he is alone. Unhappy, he searches for happiness and when he sees happiness in others he becomes angry and wants to destroy it because inside he is empty. I am not a politician, I am only a singer, but many people listen to me. I promise you that whenever I can speak on your behalf I will do

so. I shall tell your story to whomever I can because you are the only protectors of the forest and if the forest dies then so does the earth. Even a white man can understand this."

Raoni looks content.

"How did I do, J.P."

"Fine, fine."

CLOSE ENCOUNTERS OF A DEADLY KIND

After dinner we find ourselves locked inside the doctor's house with two bottles of red wine. The doctor's wife hasn't had a drink for over a year; no alcohol is allowed in the Xingu – the Indians have no resistance to it.

The white folk get pleasantly drunk on illicit plonk, we laugh a lot and I fall off a stool. There's a knock at the door and we stop laughing, hide the bottles and try to look sober as it can only be an Indian outside the door. The door is unlocked. It is Megaron, Aritana's cousin, the warden of the outpost. The doctor had left something for one of his children. He leaves and takes the air of sobriety with him. The door is quickly re-locked.

"J.P., have you ever been in any real danger here?"

"Oh yes, if you ever see the movie you'll see a scene where one of the chiefs is exhorting the killing of whites and suggesting that they should start with the film crew to show their strength. There is a close up of me looking terrified. Raoni saves us by pointing out how useful the film would be to their cause." At that moment we are interrupted by another uninvited guest: a giant green tarantula is marching straight towards me.

"Move very slowly, they jump!"

Mino and I are still in full war paint, but the tarantula isn't even remotely impressed. J.P. slowly reaches for one of the shelves and picks up an empty Maxwell House jar. He carefully unscrews the top and lowers the jar to the now stationary hairy beast. Time passes slowly, the jar moves nearer. Will he jump?

61

The Rainforest and the Greenhouse Effect

Almost all development in the Amazon involves clearing the land by burning. On a single day in 1988, scientists recorded 6,000 man-made fires burning in the Amazon. The consequences, to the forest and to the world, are devastating. As environmental concerns have shifted focus from local to global, the relationship between the burning of the rainforest and the global warming phenomenon called "the greenhouse effect" is one of the most alarming.

To some extent, the greenhouse effect is a necessary process, keeping the earth warm enough to support life. It works the same way as a gardener's greenhouse does: molecules of carbon dioxide allow the sun's rays to pass through the atmosphere – like they pass through the glass panes – and warm the earth, but the gas traps the heat by absorbing infra-red radiation. Until the industrial revolution 200 years ago, the earth's levels of carbon dioxide were regulated naturally by plants' and the ocean organisms' conversion of carbon dioxide into oxygen and carbon. Carbon is the basic building block of all organic life.

Trees felled in the tropics add to environmental warming because carbon is released into the atmosphere when the debris of a felled forest is burned or rots. Estimates suggest that one-fifth to one-third of all carbon dioxide pollution comes from tropical forest destruction, but this could rapidly increase if the Amazon rainforest continues to be burned.

Accumulating carbon dioxide is the largest single cause – about 50% – of global warming. This could result in rising sea levels, changes in world-wide weather and wind patterns, floods and droughts. Chlorofluorocarbons from plastics, aerosols and refrigeration are another major contributing factor to the greenhouse effect.

We get him. "God, he's ugly. Where's the corkscrew?"

Back in our hammocks the red dye on our bodies is apparently repugnant to mosquitos, so no net curtains tonight. A chorus of farts from our war party: "Goodnight boys!" I'm in a deep sleep, a gentle breeze rocks my hammock from side to side like a cradle. A scream wrenches me violently awake.

"Sting there's a snake. Wake up."

"Trudie you're dreaming."

"No I'm not, wake up."

I reach for the flashlight. There in front of us is an enormous snake, its head raised and poised to strike. I taste fear in my mouth, trying to shake off the nausea of drowsiness. Our bodyguards have fallen out of their hammocks by now. They see the snake and start screaming.

"Surucucu Jaca do Pico."

"Surucucu Jaca do Pico."

They run off into the jungle. We're alone with this thing.

"Did I hear right?"

"I think you did."

Mino is still in his hammock.

"Mino – are you still awake?"

"Ooski."

"Get out of the hammock very slowly, no not that side."

"Ooski."

The snake is motionless, trying to hypnotize us. I shudder when I realize that Mino and I are wearing his markings and I remember Trudie's dream. We are still, the air is cold around us. Trudie whispers, "We must move back very slowly – these fuckers can jump. It's a pit viper. One step backwards."

"Whack!" The snake has been clubbed over the head with a long stick. Our warriors have returned. Again they hit it. The snake recoils in silent agony. Again and again until the body is limp, the mouth, with its two deadly fangs, open wide and blood oozing on to the ground.

"Surucucu Jaca do Pico."

The snake moves again. "Whack!" it is dead.

J.P. and Captain Kelly have been woken by the noise. They see the snake. "My God! You are very lucky. This snake was cold. It was looking for a warm body to get next to."

The Indians are pointing to our war paint. "They say he never comes to a village. The sign on your bodies attracted him. He sacrificed himself. It will give you great power." I feel sorry for the creature, but somehow the death has punctuated our journey, given it greater validity, a heightened sense of magic

Trudie and Sting display their pit viper

and mortality. J.P. asks how we found it. "It was Trudie." Trudie looks pale and sad. "I couldn't sleep, I got up to stretch my legs, but I suddenly knew something was wrong. I turned on my flashlight and there it was at my feet, poised to strike. I turned off the light and jumped back, then I woke you. Six months ago I don't know what I would have done."

"I think you all owe your lives to Trudie," says J.P. The noise has woken up the outpost. The dead snake is greeted with awe. They begin to mark themselves with the blood of the viper.

"Powerful medicine," whispers Captain Kelly.

Don't Forget About Us

It is morning and Mino and I are in the river, attempting to wash off the war paint. Our snake is where we left him. Held at arm's length he is over six feet long. Captain Kelly has removed one of his fangs to give to me, pointing out the tiny capillary from which the poison is secreted.

We make our way to the airfield where there's a plane waiting for us and soon we are in the air high above the jungle, heading for a town called Bang-Bang where we have to catch another small plane to Brasilia. We land at Bang-Bang, so called because of the number of gunfights there, and order breakfast in a hotel/brothel while we wait for another plane.

"Well?" asks J.P.

"O.K. You were right, it was an unbelievable trip."

"Is that all? What are you going to do?"

"I'll speak to Amnesty International next week at the conference in Sao Paulo. And I want to write something."

"So long as it's not some idealistic trip about the noble savage."

"No, they are just people with human rights. It's not the noble savage I have a sense of, but the nobility of the species. My faith in man has been restored despite all the bullshit. In some ways Western man is in reverse evolution, we've forgotten our real potential. The Xingu can remind us of what we really are. They must survive."

"Here's to Raoni."

"– and the Surucucu Jaca do Pico!"

"– and the tarantula!"

"– and the panther!"

"– and the rainforest!"

"– and the rainforest!"

"Let's have breakfast. Mmm, smell that coffee."

"Ooski."

RAONI FIGHTS FOR THE FOREST

by Jean-Pierre Dutilleux

In 1973, on my first expedition into the Amazon rain-forest, I met Raoni, a chief of the Kayapo Indians. Raoni was to become one of the central figures in the Indians' fight to preserve the rainforest.

A HERO OF THE FOURTH WORLD

WHEN THE WATER BEGAN TO TASTE OF ASHES, AFTER the fish and game had dwindled to nothing, after the forest along the edge of the Xingu had been burning for months on end, it became difficult for Raoni to restrain the men of the Kayapo. They began planning for war. The time was August 1980.

Raoni is chief of the Megkronotis tribe of the Kayapo group, Indians of the southern Amazon basin in Brazil. The plate inside his distended lower lip, intended to frighten his enemies, signifies that he is a warrior by tradition. But Raoni had no wish to shed blood.

He had just returned from an expedition to Sao Paulo to buy supplies for his people: medicines, bullets for hunting, fish hooks, blankets, flashlights, and the porcelain beads the Kayapo used to make jewelery. With Raoni in Sao Paulo was a panther hunter named N'goire. It was N'goire's first trip out of the jungle, his first experience of twentieth century civilization. Without Raoni's help he wouldn't have been able to turn on a water tap or open a door. Raoni had to hold his hand so that N'goire could go downstairs or cross the street. Yet of all the strange, new sights

Keepers of the Amazon Rainforest

Far from the impenetrable, inhospitable jungles of adventure stories, the indigenous peoples see the rainforest as nurturing, not threatening. Throughout history, there have been jungle dynasties in Central Asia and Central America, whole civilizations centred in the rainforest. But unfortunately, Brazil's Indians have been fighting for their survival ever since the Portuguese first arrived in 1500. At that time, it is estimated that there were about five million Indians in Brazil. Today there are only about 200,000. Under Brazilian law, Indians are treated as wards of the state, with rights similar to minor children.

Brazil's new constitution granted Indians the right to permanent possession of the lands they inhabit, as well as exclusive use of the resources of that land. But despite a law requiring all Indian lands to be demarcated by the end of 1978, two-thirds of all tribal lands have yet to be officially marked.

N'goire found in the city, what amazed him most were the unfamiliar animals in the Sao Paulo Zoo.

Raoni, on the other hand, was no stranger to civilization, in fact he had become something of a legend. He and the Megkronotis had been the subject of my documentary film, called *Raoni*, and had been made co-producers so that they would receive a share of the profits. When payment was delayed by the film's Brazilian distributor, Raoni went to the city and banged on the company president's desk with his *borduna*, a war club, until they issued him a cheque.

The English version of the film was nominated for an Academy Award. In Brazil it was honoured as the best feature of the year and its star, Raoni, became a hero. He became an international symbol of the "Fourth World", of the indigenous people fighting for their survival against the destruction of their environment. They called him "the ecological war chief".

Raoni had no fondness for the city. "In the world of the whites everybody is afraid of everybody else," he complained. "I see poor people on the street and

Kayapo warriors preparing for war

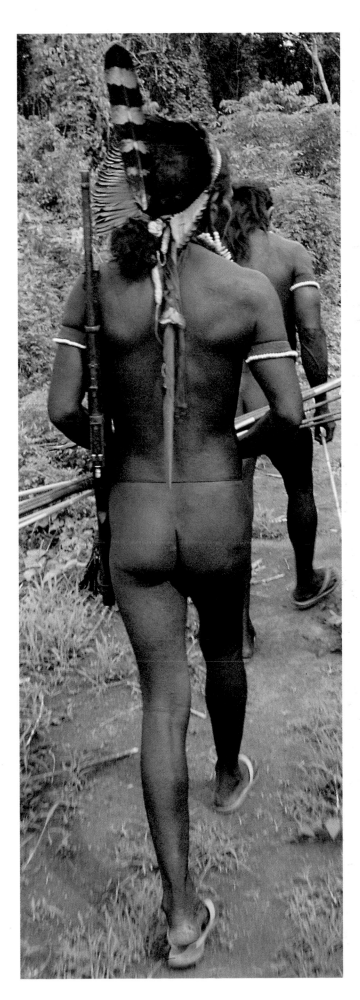

The Kayapo Indians

Two of the better-known indigenous groups remaining in the Amazon are the Kayapo and the Yanomamo. In central Brazil, the Kayapo live in the basin of the Xingu river, one of the southern tributaries of the Amazon. They practise, as part of their traditional culture, complex resource management that insures that the forest will remain healthy and diverse and therefore able to support them. In this they are typical of the indigenous people of the Amazon.

Threatened by development on the Kayapo Indian Reserve, the Kayapo have reluctantly been forced to fight for their forest, as is their right on government-designated tribal territory. The Kayapo have a tradition of warriorship and were respected as the fiercest Indians in Brazil for centuries. With the blessing of local government police, they were recently successful in demanding a percentage from 5,000 gold miners illegally prospecting on Indian lands in the Xingu.

sometimes they are Indians. They ask for money because they have nothing to eat and people pass by without looking. That's why I think money is bad. I don't want it among us. The day when Indians accept money will be the end of our life together."

He worried about the Indian learning the white man's way of life and forgetting his own way of life, his past, the stories of his ancestors. "He can't take time to live anymore, can't lie in a hammock and dream. He just keeps rushing here and there. For all these reasons we want to keep our land, so we can live the life we want."

The Desert of Ashes

On the return journey, Raoni was sickened by what he saw. Four years ago, this had been a three-hour flight over virgin rainforest. Today, where once we had skimmed the carpet of canopy, we looked down on a desert of ashes and calcinated tree trunks for two hours and forty minutes. More than half the trees

Overleaf: A meeting of the raiding party

THE YANOMAMO INDIANS

The Yanomamo, who live in the Amazon in the far north of Brazil – and in southern Venezuela – were only contacted in 1950. Unlike many other tribes, they retain most of their culture. Since the mid-1970s, however, their world has been increasingly invaded. Highway construction, mining of gold, uranium and cassiterite have brought to the Yanomamo malaria, tuberculosis, influenza, venereal disease and toxic pollution.

"The Yanomamo are being massacred as if they were not human beings," said a recent statement by Brazil's Roman Catholic Church. "Economic, political and military interests, backed by a state that should be defending the Indians, are taking precedence over the rights of the Yanomamo, whose only aspiration is to live in dignity." Despite a recent constitutional amendment recognizing the "original rights" of the Amazon's native peoples, the violation of those rights continues. Tension in the region continues to grow, with frequent violence. The army, local governments and miners frequently regard the Indians as "obstacles", the Church has been almost alone in their defence.

The National Indian Foundation, known as FUNAI, maintains however, that social and cultural integration into modern society is in the Indians' best interests. A FUNAI spokesman was recently quoted as saying, "We can't have the Indians eternally as museum pieces. Our policy is to integrate them so they can have a more human and dignified life".

Non-Indian settler population in the Amazon increased 900% between the mid-1950s and mid-1980s. All activity that brings people into the Amazon also brings diseases to which the Indians have no immunity, as well as alcohol, for which they have no tolerance. Despite promises of action, the government has been slow to evict miners and other illegal squatters from Indian lands. They have however, evicted foreign anthropologists who were helping the Indians.

gone. Nothing moved except for an occasional herd of cattle searching for the scattered tufts of grass.

Suddenly though, the rainforest appeared, so we crossed over into the Xingu National Park. The park is a reservation for the Kayapo and other groups, inside which the Indians have jurisdiction. The virgin forest was a majestic sight bathed in the morning sun, with sheets of mist still clinging to the tree tops. The pilot flew low to look for the village, following the course of one river, then another. Raoni spotted the village first.

On the village's makeshift landing strip, Raoni handed out the gifts he had brought. Many of the Indians were crying because they had missed him so much.

Eventually, the women returned to the manioc plantations. The men went off to hunt or fish. Children were practising their archery. Raoni noticed that work was already under way repairing a roof that had caved in. The huts of the village housed up to thirty people each. It might take as long as six months to constuct one but they lasted for about fifteen years. Raoni was glad to be home.

THE BUILD-UP OF TENSION

In the men's lodge, in the centre of the village, Raoni was brought up to date on the situation with the farmers. There would be trouble as long as there were still Indians resisting "the tide of progress".

There was no real political authority within the tribe. As chief, Raoni had no power of repression or unilateral decision; he could only advise. Because of the film, his prestige and therefore his power of persuasion had increased with all of the Kayapo. It was unlikely, however, that they would be dissuaded from this fight.

Raoni had already tried to warn the men who were invading their land, razing and burning the trees for farmland that would only be fertile for a few years.

"This land has always been ours. And in any case, the government had deeded it to us," he told them. "Don't log any further or you won't be returning."

To his own people, he advised patience. "We are too few. By ourselves, we will die. I will talk to the other tribes first, because we have to unite before we can fight. I also want to talk to the president of FUNAI. Maybe I can get him to clarify the frontiers that we were promised years ago."

He appealed to FUNAI, the government's Indian Affairs Foundation. FUNAI had a new president, a man with a good reputation. His staff were people who meant well for the people of the jungle. FUNAI was making a considerable effort on their behalf in the face of difficult pressures from other factions in the government and business in Brazil. Over the years, scores of FUNAI employees had died protecting the Indians.

> *"If we lose our land the white man will destroy the whole forest. And then, where will we go to hunt the tapir, the ant bear, the panther? What will we eat when there is no game left?"*

Part of FUNAI's responsibility was demarcation of the borders of the Indian lands with a cleared frontier six yards wide. This they had been woefully slow to finish, and without obvious borders it was easy for greedy miners and desperate homesteaders to cross into Indian lands and then claim ignorance.

"If we lose our land the whites will destroy the whole forest," Raoni said. "And then, where will we go to hunt the tapir, the ant bear, the panther? What will we eat when there is no game left?" FUNAI promised to finish demarcation of the tribal lands, but work on the boundary stalled in the rainy season. Meanwhile the woodcutters went on clearing and burning the forest.

The Indians were angry.

Alone, Raoni went to the loggers one more time. "This is our land," he said. "I warn you: if you stay, my people will come and kill you."

But he was wasting his time. The bulldozers roared into life again, pulling the giant chains that can waste up to a hundred hectares of forest a day. Raoni could hear the engines deep in the forest. The diesel fumes overpowered the familiar smells of the soil and the river. The animals fled.

AN ERUPTION OF VIOLENCE

Raoni radioed FUNAI and warned that violence, war with the whites, was inevitable. Legally, this was Indian land and the Kayapo had the legal right to fight to defend it.

The Megkronotis were joined by men from other tribes: the Suya, Juruna and Kajabi tribes. The warriors put on their black paint and took up their bows, clubs and guns. "Don't kill the woodcutters," Raoni said. "Just hit them hard enough to give them a real fright and put them off returning." With a sinking heart, he watched the men set out.

The Indians stole across the ashes and attacked the woodcutter's camp with lightning speed. The loggers were disarmed and stripped before they could draw their guns.

"Why don't you let us get on with our work?" one of them cried. "You're all a bunch of bums and idlers!"

One of the Indians, whose cousin had been killed by workers on a nearby farm a few months before, lost his temper. He lashed out with his club, hitting harder and harder. The others joined in. The accumulated rage of centuries was vented on the woodcutters. With brutal savagery they struck, in revenge for all the Indians who had died or suffered since the white man had come to the forest; for the individuals, for the

tribes, for the entire nations that had been massacred in murderous attacks, or infected with diseases to which they had no resistance.

> "I want to trust the government. I keep hoping that they will set down our frontiers once and for all. If not, the fighting will go on and they will have to kill us down to the last Indian. Then there will be no more Indians left, and no problem, either."

And their anger came from shame. Shame at the ridicule they received for going naked, or not earning money. And most of all for the shame they felt for the Indians who had become "integrated" – loaded into trucks like cattle and crammed into shanty towns in the cities where they became "good Indians" because now they were exploitable and their land could be taken, and where they worked for nothing until they died of tuberculosis or alcoholism.

Eleven of the workers were bludgeoned to death that day with Kayapo war clubs. (The Kayapo do not use their guns on humans.) The dead were illiterate peasants, clearing the forest for a living because they had their own families to feed. And they were half-Indian.

Not long after the attack on the logging camp, the same group sank the barge which ferried trucks across the Xingu River on the road to Manaus.

Two weeks later the men of Gorotire, another Kayapo village, launched their own attack. Twenty-one died.

Previous page: Armed warriors moving through
an area of burned-out forest
Left: The woodcutters are bludgeoned to death
by Kayapo warriors

Then the Xavante Indians destroyed a bridge on the Araguaia River to stop the stream of immigrants who had fled starvation conditions in Nordeste in the hope of a better life in the Amazon, even if that better life was at the expense of the rainforest's indigenous people.

Sixty miles from the Xingu was the town of Bang-Bang, a rough frontier town reminiscent of the American West. There the whites' anger, too, swelled with hate and violence.

"Indians and pigs are the same thing," said one farmer. "If either one comes on my land, I don't think twice. I kill them."

The Indians were getting away with murder, the townspeople said, because they were protected by the State. "They've got to be taught a lesson," someone else suggested. "A lot of people are going to get killed around here if FUNAI doesn't make up its mind."

> "Indians and pigs are the same thing," said one farmer. "If either one comes on my land, I don't think twice. I kill them."

CONFIRMATION OF RIGHTS

But when FUNAI did make up its mind, it was in favour of the Indians. The Interior Minister of the time affirmed that all the lands inhabited by the Indians belonged to the Indians, and so did the resources those lands produced. He said that the farmers had been warned not to set foot on those lands, so the deaths would not alter the government's policy on the rainforest's native inhabitants.

More importantly, the Minister announced plans for a buffer zone of forest nine miles wide, between whites and Indians. He threatened to create a FUNAI police force if necessary. They would evacuate all non-Indians inside the reservation and complete

clearing of the park's boundaries by the end of the year.

It was a major victory for the Indians. But would it prove to be only temporary?

Other Kayapo remained suspicious, but Raoni said, "I want to trust them. I will tell my men to stop killing other farmers. I keep hoping that won't be necessary any longer, and that the government will set down our frontiers once and for all. If not, the fighting will go on and they will have to kill us down to the last Indian. Then there will be no more Indians left, and no problem, either."

RAONI
MEETS
RED CROW

by Jean-Pierre Dutilleux

The problems of the Indians in the Amazon are similar to those experienced by the North American Indians. Raoni wished to meet Indian representatives from the United States. In 1979, I asked Floyd 'Red Crow' Westerman, a Dakota-Sioux Indian, to come and visit his cousins of the rainforest. Red Crow accepted, but he had to wait until January 1987 to be allowed to come to Brazil . . .

A LONG AWAITED VISIT

AT THE AIRPORT IN RIO, AN UNUSUAL PASSENGER WAITED to clear customs on January 13, 1987. He was tall and solidly built, wearing a fringed shirt, jeans and a cowboy belt, with his long grey hair in two plaits. He carried only a small grip and a chamois bag on his chest. His American passport listed his birthplace as the Dakota Reservation in South Dakota and had dozens of stamps. When the inspector asked him what was in the chamois bag, Floyd Westerman, better known by his Dakota-Sioux name of Red Crow, was not to be intimidated.

"Sacred object," he said.

Impressed, the officer let him pass without further inspection.

I was waiting for him. We have been old friends since the Native American march on Washington in

Red Crow, chief of the Dakota-Sioux Indians
from North America

1979 and had been planning this trip for a long time. The 1979 march had taken place in protest against a proposed law to do away with the reservations. Taking away "Mother Earth" from an Indian would mean his spiritual death, as all his religion is connected to the land of his ancestors.

Since this was Red Crow's first visit to Brazil, I gave him a tour. On the beaches, he watched the half-naked bodies tanning under the tropical sun. By Ipanema, he laughed and said, "It's hard to be a spiritual man in Rio."

That night, he sat alone for a long time, meditating under the full moon.

Red Crow is an Indian activist in the guise of a troubador, wandering the United States and the world to sing his songs about the traditions and struggles of his people. On reservations and in the city slums, he gives what courage he can to his brothers fighting poverty and alcoholism.

Red Crow sees Raoni's struggle as identical with that of the North American Indians a century ago. He thinks of Raoni as a 20th century Sitting Bull.

It was Red Crow's belief that only Indian spirituality could save the men and the tribes from degeneration. He himself had taken part in eight sun dances to purify himself; dancing for four days in the sun without food or water around his tree, connected to it by a rope tied to pieces of wood inserted under his skin.

To the Indians, the tree was a relative, the same way all four-legged and all winged things were relatives. "If we don't treat it that way," Red Crow would say, "we are missing an important connection".

Yet in the Amazon, they were killing the trees. And at the long-standing invitation of the Kayapo chief, Raoni, Red Crow had come to meet his distant cousins in the jungle. He was coming as if he was the first North American Indian to visit Amazonia since the migration of tribes separated them a hundred thousand years ago.

The visit had been a long time coming. I had conveyed Raoni's invitation at a showing of my documentary, *Raoni*, to the chiefs of the Navajo, Cheyenne, Hopi and Yellow Feet tribes when they reached Washington on their march.

Red Crow had been fascinated, accepting the invitation and sending gifts for the Amazonian Indians. Raoni had sent presents to Red Crow in return and applied to the government for permission for the Sioux's visit. At the time, however, Brazil was still ruled by a military junta and Raoni already had a growing reputation as a "troublesome Indian". The request was refused.

It was only after democratic government had been restored in Brazil in 1985 that there was any hope for the trip. Finally, after seven years, Red Crow was granted a visa.

TRAVELLING TO THE FOREST

Red Crow and I flew to Brasilia the day after his arrival in Rio. This time journalists were waiting for us at the airport, and Red Crow held tightly to the chamois bag while he answered questions.

A car was put at his disposal by the FUNAI, the government department responsible for the country's remaining 220,000 indigenous people. The next day, Red Crow met with the president of FUNAI and gave him an eagle feather.

A day later, Red Crow met with Brazil's Minister of the Interior. Reporters and news cameramen, who had been following him everywhere in the capital, filled the room. Red Crow smiled and took a few sage leaves from his pocket, put them in the minister's ashtray and set fire to them.

"That's to chase away the evil spirits," he said. Then he turned and said an incantation to the four directions of the wind. Camera flashes popped; mouths fell open.

That night Globo, Brazil's largest television network, devoted ten full minutes to the meeting on the evening news. It showed the minister promising to mark out 150 reservations. Then it showed Red Crow offering the official another of his eagle feathers. The eagle is the bird which flies highest, Red Crow explained, and therefore, according to Indian belief it is closest to the creator.

Brazilian papers repeated the story on their front pages the next morning. By then, Red Crow was on his way in the minister's plane, heading for the Amazon rainforest.

The first stop was a town called Bang-Bang, so named because of its reputation for trigger-happy *pistoleiros*. We needed to pick up supplies for the Kayapo; rice, beans, batteries for flashlights, hammocks, fishing line. The Kayapo lack everything. We also bought 25 pounds of blue and white beads as presents for our hosts, the favourite colours of the Tchucaramae, the Kayapo nation.

The Cessna took off again for the frontier of the Xingu, the region named after a tributary of the Amazon. It is a territory larger than Belgium and is entirely under Indian control. The border had only been demarcated two years before, by bulldozers cutting a 30-yard border all the way around the 1,000-mile perimeter of the reservation. The demarcation was an important step in claiming jurisdiction over the land.

We landed on a dirt airstrip near an Indian "vigilance post", where three Indian customs officials presided over non-Indian traffic through the reservation. Every day they controlled the flow of gold-hunters on the single road through the reservation, collecting a toll from the *carimpeiros*. The miners are not allowed to stop until they reach the other side of the Kayapo territory. The officials at the post also keep a lookout for poachers and mahogany collectors.

Today, of course, was a break from the routine. They had been told of Red Crow's arrival by radio from Brasilia and had been waiting to welcome the now-famous Sioux who was to spend his first night in the Amazon at their post.

Red Crow was impressed by the rainforest. He was struck by the sense of "breathing" he felt night and day as the sun, clouds and rain came and went in the constant humidity. "My lungs felt good to be there," he said afterwards. "It felt healthy to be in such a pure place."

"It's sad that this world is in such a fierce, intense rush towards destruction, and taking the indigenous tribes with it."

A VISIT TO THE KREEN-AKAORES

The next day, the 18th, we headed down the Xingu River in one of the reservation's only motorboats. Beyond the banks, the jungle was dense: opaque, noisy and mysterious. To Red Crow, this forest had an extra, profound meaning.

"Anthropologists say we all come from the Bering Strait. That's not *our* story," he said. The Sioux believe that they, unlike some of the other North American Indian tribes, actually came from South America, descended from the same ancestors as groups like the Kayapo. "We were born out of the jungles. My going back down was reconnecting with our ancestors."

After three hours, we put ashore so we could visit my old friends the Kreen-Akaores, the "giant Indians".

The Kreen-Akaores' history is a sad one. Barely ten years ago, they had their first contact with white men – and almost perished because of it. The Trans-Amazonian, the great highway that cuts across Brazil, was going to cut through the Kreen-Akaores' territory. And large landholders were appropriating slices of the forest on either side.

91

The Villas-Boas brothers, Brazilian anthropologists and pioneers in the defence of Indian rights, spent four years tracking the tribe so they could be prepared for contact with other white men, who would be less sensitive to their needs. They convinced the tribe of about 250 to move to the Xingu Reservation where they would be safe. But the move itself, which was carried out by plane, was a shock. In a matter of months, all but 60 of the Kreen-Akaores had died, victims of malaria, smallpox and measles, to which they had no resistance. Some simply died from being removed from their homeland.

Since then, however, thanks to the aid and protection of the Kayapo, their numbers had recovered to over 100 again. It was a miracle; unique in the history of Brazilian tribes. Their culture survived the shock of transplant largely intact, but for one notable exception: they now had their own football team.

MEETING WITH RAONI

After another four hours on the river, we finally docked at Kapoto, a new village Raoni had built a year before in the middle of land recently granted them by Brasilia. A few Tchucaramae warriors, painted entirely in black, were waiting for us. With them was Megaron, Raoni's nephew, whom I had known since my first trip into the rainforest in 1973.

Red Crow stood silent.

"Raoni is waiting for you in the men's hut," Megaron told me in a solemn tone.

I followed him up from the bank to the village, where low huts of woven branches covered with straw formed a circle almost a mile in diameter. The village

The historic meeting between Raoni and Red Crow, Indian chiefs from North and South America

appeared deserted. The women and children had fled at the sound of the outboard.

The men's hut stood in the centre of the circle, the place where Tchucaramae men met to discuss tribal business, plan attacks, settle conflicts, or just to get away from the women and children to smoke and tell jokes. A sort of local men's club.

Inside, Raoni got out of his hammock to embrace me. During the filming of the 1979 documentary, when other Indian warriors wanted to kill the film crew as an example to the whites invading their land, Raoni had spoken for us and saved our lives.

"I have brought you the Indian, Red Crow the Sioux, as you asked me to," I said.

"Ah," said Raoni, from behind the wooden plate embedded in his lower lip. "So you came with the Indian!" He said it as if it were a mild surprise. As if he hadn't been planning the visit for ten years and expecting Red Crow for a week now.

"Where is he!"

"Outside."

Raoni went and stood at the entrance to the men's hut, with the other Tchucaramae chiefs behind him. All of them were painted black.

Red Crow crossed the clearing still carrying the chamois bag, approaching to look his counterparts in the eye. Red Crow's had tears in them.

"I've been waiting for you a long time," Raoni said. "I want to get to know you. I have many things to say to you." "I come in the name of my tribe," the Sioux responded. He touched the chamois gently. "I have brought the sacred pipe of my people. It is the symbol of my people."

"I hope others will come."

"I am the first, the pathfinder. Many others will come."

Red Crow presenting the sacred pipe of his tribe to the Tchucaramae Indians

Back in the men's hut, I interpreted the endless dialogue.

Red Crow recounted stories of his ancestors: the adventures of Cochise and Sitting Bull. He explained how the pipe he had brought, still in the chamois bag, was similar to the one those two had smoked with the U.S. Army General George Custer a century ago to celebrate the signing of treaties the white men never respected.

Raoni countered with many tales of the Kayapo's warrior tradition. For over half a century, the Kayapo had dominated an area of rainforest larger than that of France.

Red Crow proposed the construction of a sweat lodge and Raoni sent ten warriors into the forest to work under the Sioux's direction. In an hour they were ready with a hut of branches and leaves, designed to trap the air inside.

The Ceremonial Pipe

Red Crow put on his mocassins and his ceremonial vest. Raoni and a few other chiefs joined him inside. For the first time since he had arrived in Brazil, Red Crow removed the wooden pipe from its bag. The tobacco came from the underbark of the red willow, harvested in the winter from Red Crow's native South Dakota.

After his incantation to the four winds, he lit the pipe, inhaled deeply and sent up the smoke, where it mixed with the smoke of the fire. After a few pulls, he passed the pipe to Raoni. Both North and South American Indians use smoke to dispel evil spirits. The Kayapo, however, were used neither to the pipe, nor to the sweet tobacco, tasting of bark steeped in honey. Raoni savoured a long puff, then passed the pipe around, remaining meditative.

When the pipe returned to him, Red Crow began another incantation. Then he placed stones heated in the fire on the floor in the centre of the sweat lodge. Suddenly, he emptied a bucket on the rocks; the

National Sovereignty

Nationalism in Latin America is an important consideration. For a long time, it seems, Brazil thought of its impenetrable interior not so much as resource but as a challenge, almost a national shame because of its formidableness. Moreover, Brazilians respond to criticism by pointing out that Europe and North America's rise to industrial power was fuelled by the decimation of its own forests.

"Every time someone in the U.S. says the Amazon belongs to mankind, it becomes more difficult to have a rational discussion," said a government official in a recent newspaper story.

In recent years, international environmental groups have sponsored "debt-for-nature swamps", in which industrial world lending institutions sell the debts to the conservation groups at a discount. They in turn forgive some of a country's debts in exchange for guarantees of conservation. While other South American countries have taken advantage of the plan, Brazil has largely considered offers to trade some of its $121 billion international debt for environmental protection to be offensive to its national sovereignty. The United States, France, West Germany, Japan and the Netherlands had all offered to trade some of their notes for nature.

Like many developing countries – which have no wish to remain "developing countries" – Brazil frequently uses their international debts as justification for the over-exploitation of national natural resources like tropical forests. But in fact, while the Amazon takes up two thirds of Brazil's territory, it accounts for only three percent of that country's gross national product.

Another political factor is that the Brazilian military has long considered its national security to depend on occupation of the forest. Almost twenty years ago, when the country was run by the military, government policy spurred settlement and development of the rainforest. Nominal civilian rule returned to Brazil only in 1985, and this policy is only just beginning to give way. As late as 1985, however, Brazil's National Security Council claimed that pro-Indian groups were trying to create a Yanomamo Republic which would occupy parts of both Brazil and Venezuela. They used this as further justification for establishment of bases and settlements in the north.

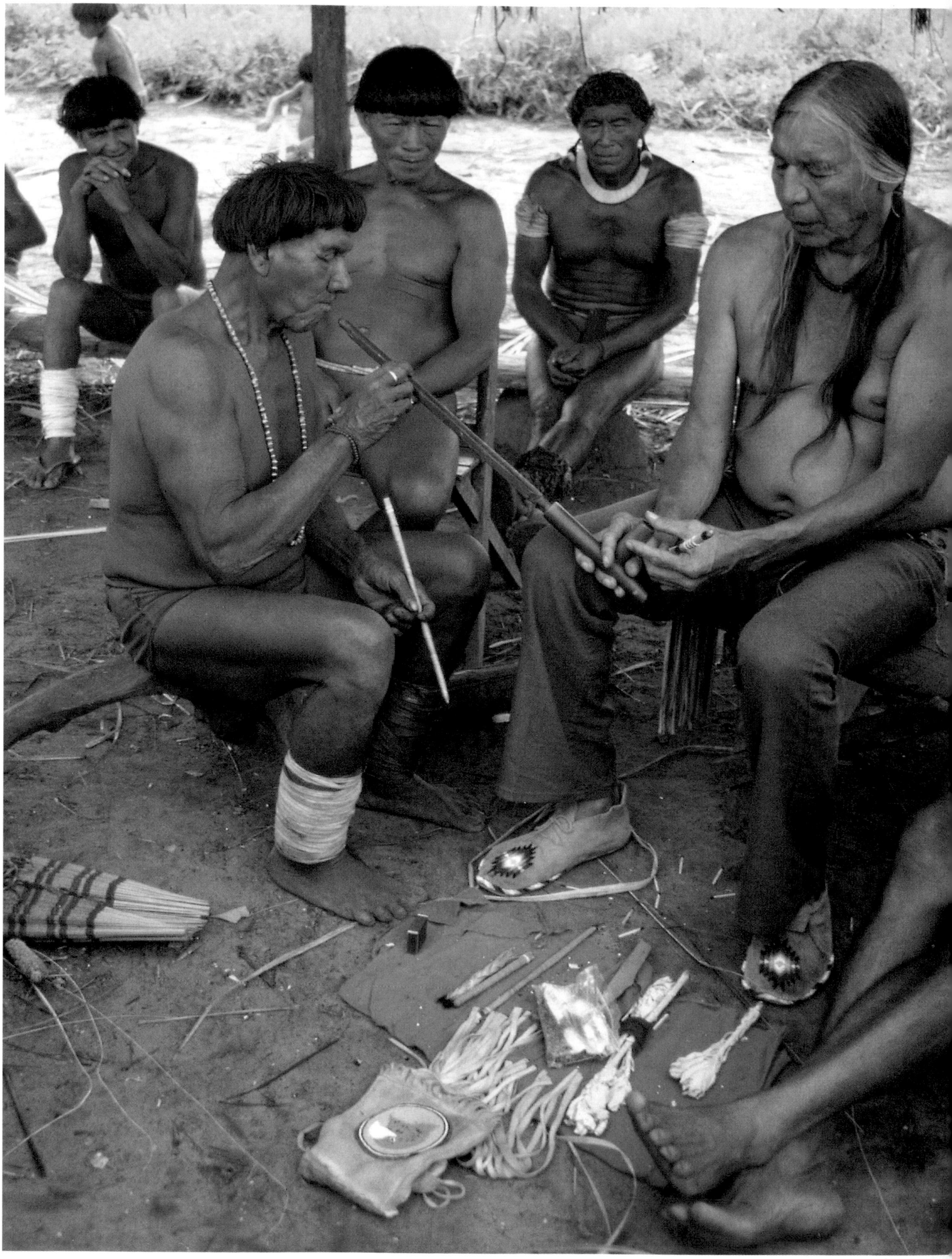

water turned immediately to steam and the hut became almost unbearably hot.

"This purifies the soul," Red Crow explained.

Despite the unaccustomed discomfort, the Kayapo did not want to lose face by leaving. The ritual continued until nightfall. Then Raoni invited Red Crow to sleep in his hut, where the whole family hung in hammocks, one above the other.

Red Crow learned from the Kayapo that an entire tribe, with no previous contact with the whites, had been murdered by large landholders near the Bolivian border. They were lured with gifts, then cut down by machine guns and buried in an unmarked mass grave.

The next day, Red Crow officially donated the pipe to the Tchucaramae. The most important warriors, still painted black and wearing head-dresses of parrot feathers, formed a circle around Red Crow. Incanting in the Sioux language to the four directions of the wind, he first lifted the pipe to the Great Spirit, then placed it on the shoulder of each warrior. Then he lit the pipe one last time and handed it to Raoni, along with the bag, herbs, tobacco and pipe cleaner.

Raoni held it to his heart, then he crowned Red Crow with a head-dress of Arara feathers.

BROTHERS IN ARMS

Red Crow spent two more days in Kapoto. He was astounded by the malaria, pneumonia and amoebic dysentery that afflicted the Indians, by the scorpions, snakes, mosquitos and even by the rain. "I almost never slept," he confessed to me. "Cockroaches hanging in swarms on the ceiling fell onto my face and

cleaned themselves inside the wounds of my mosquito bites. I would never have thought living in the jungle could be so difficult."

Red Crow and Raoni spent hours talking about old traditions, the ceremonies they had exchanged and the importance of their new contact. Red Crow felt honoured to have shared the sweat lodge with the Tchucaramae. He noted that the Kayapo, too, had a tradition of building a closed hut in the jungle for communion with the spirit world, even though they did not fill it with steam. He noted that the two Indians, from such seemingly different worlds, prayed to the creator in the same manner. That was more of a connection than anything else. "Their spiritual beliefs are the most important part of their life," he said. "And the way we held the ceremonies was so similar that one could see the connection, the same beliefs for 100 million Indians, from Canada all the way down to South America."

The Kayapo told him about the ranchers' hunting parties for Indians. Government policy allowed Brazilians to homestead in any area where there weren't any Indians. It was a familiar line to Red Crow. "The same thing happened to us in the 1850s when the first wagon trains were going across South Dakota. The government said you could homestead if there were no Indians there. But that was our backyard." This was the Amazonian Indians' backyard. "They're just going in and killing the Indians off and then saying that there are no Indians. The homesteading is just land theft."

Raoni said, "I'm glad that you came to be with me, to know that you stand with us and we can fight together in this struggle to save our way of life."

Red Crow and I loaded the boat and set off along the Xingu for the vigilance post.

ARITANA'S VILLAGE

The post of Leonardo had been named for one of the Villas-Boas brothers. It was the meeting place of the Upper Xingu. In the plain below sixteen Indian groups of different languages and tribal nationalities lived together in harmony. The native peoples of the rainforest no longer fought amongst themselves. Here at the source of the Xingu they were protected from poachers, gold-seekers and the bulldozers of the Trans-Amazonian; protected by the Suyas and Tchucaramae warriors around them, who had the right to defend their territory – by force if necessary. The post, built where the jungle was less dense, was home to a dozen people including nurses, teachers and even a cook. A few children from each tribe attended school there to learn reading, writing, arithmetic and about the world of the whites. This was how the chiefs prepared their future ranks of lawyers and delegates to represent the Indians.

The chief of the post, an Iaualapiti Indian, invited Red Crow to come to his village a few miles away, by bicycle. Not having been on a bike in years, the Sioux was ill at ease.

The Iaualapiti form a tribe with many *pajés*, or sorcerers. They rarely meet with the whites. Red Crow and I settled under a small shelter in the centre of the village and smoked long cigars with the Iaualapiti's chief, Aritana.

"Below us, all the dead of the village are buried," Aritana said. "They are among us."

In the spreading darkness, men were returning one by one from the forest. All of them were painted

103

BRAZIL ACTS

As national awareness grows, public opinion in Brazil is beginning to change. Brazil's Green Party has formed a grass roots, ecological voting block. Under pressure from foreign environmental groups, governments and international lending agencies, the Brazilian government, too, is beginning to take action. In October, 1988, Brazilian President José Sarney announced steps to slow the destruction of the Amazon, promising to reverse a twenty-eight-year policy of "conquering" the jungle through growth and development. Sarney promised the government would suspend incentives and tax breaks for development that harmed the environment. Cattle ranching, for instance, depends on government subsidies to be economically viable. Brazil also subsidizes dams, mines, road building, and all the settlement that goes along with such major projects. The president ordered studies to determine which areas should be used for cattle and agriculture and which should be preserved.

By February of 1989, however, Brazil's new plans to protect the environment were endangered by budget cuts only four months after their conception. In a surprise move – and a major change of policy – Brazil allowed that it would accept international funds to support protection of the Amazon, as long as conservation projects remain under Brazilian control.

with red urvcu dye; they were all sorcerers, the chief explained. Generally the *pajés* were healers, but when they wanted to harm someone they could mix some sacred herbs into some food, then bury the mixture in the forest. A few days later, the victim was dead. But if the victim's family identified the *pajé* he might soon be dead as well, his head smashed by an Iaualapiti war club.

Aritana explained some of their other customs. The Iaualapiti use smoke for healing.

"We too," said the Sioux.

The Iaualapiti love smoking their long cigars to chase away the evil spirits at the end of the day.

"We use pipes for that." Red Crow said.

Aritana talked until well into the night. He told of visiting sacred places where rivers flowing into the Amazon have their source. Spirits appear there.

"Last week I saw a *bandeirantes*, one of the first conquerors of Brazil. He was on horseback, in full armour, galloping across a lake."

CONFRONTATION

Red Crow returned to Leonardo to find himself in the middle of an Indian crisis. Some of the Kayapo chiefs flew back to Brasilia with him to threaten the president of FUNAI.

"If they build the eight dams planned on our land, we will attack," one of them warned.

The FUNAI official was conciliatory. "This project will never be carried out as long as I am president," he said. But knowing his position's high rate of turnover, this was small comfort to the Indians.

"And the hole, there, in the Serra of Cachimbo? If they keep on with it I'll attack it," said another.

Now the Indians were really furious, and rightly so. In the very centre of Kayapo territory, the army had built a top-secret base and had dug a huge hole. Two highly explosive rumours were circulating at the time: it would be the site of Brazil's first nuclear weapon test; or it would be used to bury nuclear waste. In the event of an accident in either case, the largest river system in the world could become radio-active. Ironically, the Indians were the only ones to intervene.

Red Crow learned from the Kayapo chiefs that an entire tribe, with no previous contact with the whites, had been murdered by large landholders. In Rondonia, near the Bolivian border, they were lured with gifts, then cut down by machine guns and buried in an unmarked, mass grave. They told him about chiefs who sold out to the mining companies, trading their people's future for cash and airplanes.

"It's very sad that that has to happen. It's sad that the people of Brazil are so poor that they have no place else to go except to look for any job there is, even if it's as dehumanizing as gold mining," Red Crow observed. "It's sad that this world is in such a fierce, intense rush towards destruction, and taking the indigenous cultures with it."

He added, "I believe people will come to a place where they realize the results of this kind of great destruction. Whether it will be in time to save the lives of future generations, I don't know."

But the fact that the Indians could speak of this

Red Crow performs a sacred ritual in the demarcation area

with him at all was a hopeful sign of changing times in democratized Brazil. Now, Indian chiefs from around the country could come to Brasilia to defend their interests. They even organized a collective demonstration in front of the President of the Republic to protest their lack of representation in the Congress.

Maintaining the Spiderweb of Life

In Brasilia, the tribal chiefs welcomed Red Crow with embraces, compliments and invitations. Brazil's President, José Sarney, at work on his country's new constitution, sent his compliments.

As a delegate of the International Indian Treaty Council, an important Native American organization, Red Crow had made many trips to Geneva to meet with international organizations. He warned his cousins about this new constitution.

"You have to ask for two things," he said. "First is the right to religion, which is connected with the recognition of sacred lands. Moreover, the constitution must forbid any government to decrease the Indian lands," he said. "If not, you will lose everything, bit by bit."

Red Crow had made this first trip. He had been the pathfinder. He'd begun the process of restoring the connections between the indigenous people of North and South America. And connections were what it was all about.

The Garden of Humanity

In the time it has taken you to read this chapter, perhaps 600,000 trees have been cut down in rainforests around the world.

Nobody can predict exactly what's going to happen; estimates vary. But it is becoming pretty obvious that the odds are against us if we insist on playing the most dangerous game of gambling with our planet while corporations focus on short-term profits and individuals focus on short-term survival.

Heat waves, droughts, floods and hurricanes are only the beginning. Humanity is remarkably adaptable. As peoples try to adjust, however, the world will see social, economic and political chaos from the most dramatic and rapid climatic changes in human experience.

The rate of devastation in the Amazon rainforest is increasing geometrically and, with no action, it is likely the rainforest will all be gone in as little as fifty years – except for the enclaves we can protect.

The survival of the Indians and the survival of the rainforest are one and the same. A few decades ago, this wasn't necessarily so, because there was so much forest. Now, one protects the other. Now, in a sense, we must realize that we are all children of the rainforest. We are all nourished and protected by it. And we are all charged with the responsibility of tending its garden. It is a global problem and requires global solutions.

We must all become keepers of the forest.

"As Indians on this continent, we have thousand-year-old teachings that tell us that all life is connected – a spiderweb of life from the insects all the way to the eagles in the sky. And what we do to one strand, we do to the whole spiderweb," he said. "It's this connection that the world has to begin to learn and to see in order to live right on earth."

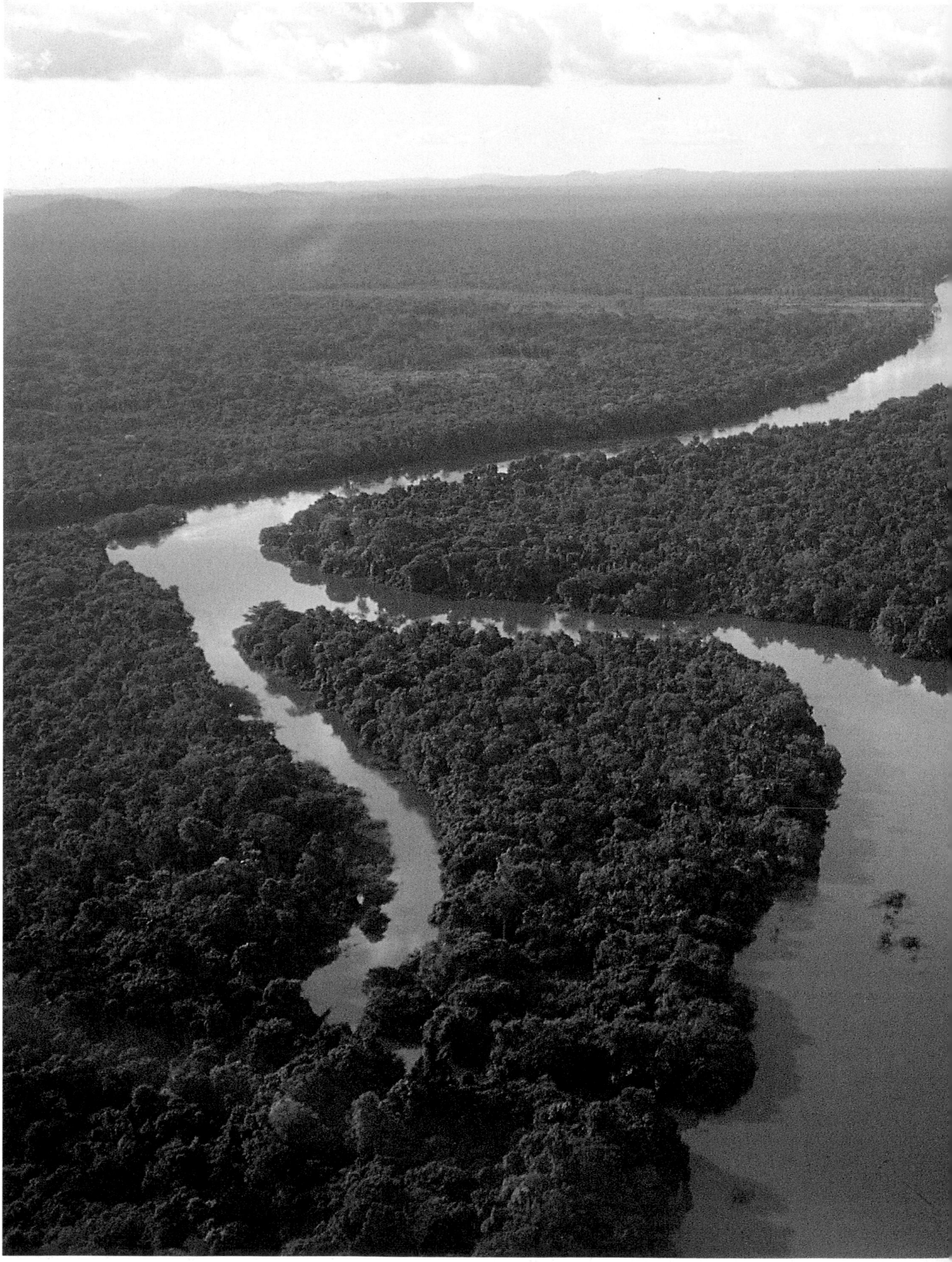

LETTER FROM ALTAMIRA

by Sting

In February 1989 I returned to Brazil, accompanied by Jean-Pierre Dutilleux and Red Crow, with three aims. We hoped to persuade President Sarney to agree to our plans for a Rainforest Foundation; we needed passports for Raoni and Megaron to join our tour of the developed countries to raise funds for the Foundation; and we had agreed to fly Raoni to Altamira to take part in an Indian protest against a planned dam.

A DREAM OF THE FOREST

THERE ARE DREAMS THAT ARE TOO REAL, THEY POSSESS an ultra reality, painted in the vivid primary colours of life and death, so galvanising that your waking life can seem like a waiting room where your heartbeat is but the prose of a ticking clock, endured only until you can return to the dream.

The Amazon is such a dream, a dream that calls you back to the womb of the forest. As I write this aboard our tiny aircraft, the radio crackles into life and tells us in tones of panic that our second plane, carrying our film crew, has crashed-landed in the jungle. It is at this point that I realise how quickly the dream of the Amazon can become a nightmare.

It was over a year since my last visit, when I sat in a jungle clearing with Raoni, the Kayapo chieftain, as he drew a crude map of the Xingu river in the sand. He pointed out three existing Indian reservations and spoke of his own dream to join these reservations with the vast unexplored area of the protected National Park. He was enlisting my help as a public figure, as well as that of Jean-Pierre Dutilleux, a film maker and long-time Indian activist and also an old friend. Raoni had saved his life not once, but twice. For J.P., when Raoni asks for help, he has no choice, there is a debt to pay. "How can we help?"

"I need money to set up the park physically with clear borders, and I need the world to know of its existence so it can survive."

Although Raoni looks like a fearsome stone age warrior with his lip plate and war paint, he has a pure intelligence that burns in his eyes and in the clarity of his thoughts.

"Inside this unexplored region there are a number of groups who have never been contacted by the white man", he said. "When they are, they are in mortal danger from disease, the destruction of their land, even murder. Every year, the burning of the forest by the white settler gets closer and closer. You must help me stop it or there will be no forest left."

And so we are returning to Brazil to make real the first stage of Raoni's dream. We need the permission of the government to allow us to take Raoni and his nephew Megaron to Europe and North America to raise funds to set up the park. Joining J.P. and myself are a French film crew and the chief of the Dakota Sioux, the Ambassador of the International Indian Treaty Council, Red Crow. Red Crow sees Raoni's struggle as identical with that of the North American Indians a century ago. He thinks of Raoni as the new Sitting Bull.

MEETING WITH THE MINISTER

It is Saturday, 18th February 1989; we are on the roof of the San Marco Hotel in Brasilia. I have a heavy cold which I must lose before we visit the Indians. The sun is shining over the distant mountains. Red Crow is performing the ceremony of the four directions, an Indian prayer for the success of our mission. He calls on the spirit world of the north, east, south and west to look kindly on our enterprise. The sky glows gold in front of us, the full moon at our backs and to the west, over the distant jungle, a flash of lightning. The

In November 1988, Raoni appeared with Sting at the opening of the Amnesty International World Tour in Sao Paulo. On stage, Raoni painted Sting in traditional Kayapo fashion. Later, Sting, Dutilleux and Raoni discussed the goals of the Rainforest Foundation. Specifically, the incorporation of three existing Indian reservations – as well as the lands between them – into one, larger National Park.

ceremony has a simple dignity and we need all the help we can get for tonight. We are to meet Fernando Mesquita, a close political advisor of President Sarney himself.

Brasilia is a ghost town at the weekends, with most of the government workers escaping to the beaches of Rio. Fernando Mesquita is at home in his apartment in the suburbs. It is a warm evening and a few children are playing outside.

He opens the door himself and invites us into his small living room and thanks us for coming. Seeing that I have a cold, his wife offers to make me a drink of bourbon, lemon and Brazilian honey, which I gratefully accept. Mr. Mesquita then begins to tell us of the problems that Brazil faces.

"There are more slum dwellers in one *favella* in Rio than all the Indians in Brazil. The poor move to the forest of the north out of desperation. If jobs could be provided in the cities, they would stay there."

"But why is a country of such a size and with such resources so economically backward?"

"The answer is simple, international debts: 17 billion dollars is sent to the banks of the developed world every year, and this is only to service the debt. Frankly," he says, "Brazil will never be able to pay off this debt. The rules are too strict. It is economic slavery. Our country has a trade surplus and yet this onus of debt cripples us. Inflation is rampant and instead of creating the one million jobs that the economy needs to provide, the poor are forced out into the countryside, decimating Brazil's natural resources for their own survival."

"What if the debt was removed or the repayment rules were relaxed?"

"Then we might have some chance of getting on our feet."

"What if you declared a moratorium on the debt like they did in Peru?"

"Then we would be ostracised from the international financial community. Our economy produces cruzados, we need dollars to buy certain goods essential for our development. We were crippled in the past

by payments to the King of Portugal, now we are slaves to the banks."

"How much is the debt?"

"One billion dollars."

"When did you borrow this?"

"Mainly in the 1970s."

"Why?"

"The banks themselves encouraged us. It was the time of the first oil shortages. The banks were desperate for somewhere to put their money. It is very easy to fall into debt when money is so available." The root of all our problems, poverty, pollution, destruction of the forest, the birthrate, is a function of the debt. We are powerless in the face of it. Appease the banks and we can save the rainforests."

We outline for the minister our modest plan to create a Xingu National Park with privately raised funds in Europe, North America and Japan, and express our desire to work in partnership with the Brazilian government. Can he help us, and most importantly, can the minister organise a meeting between ourselves and President Sarney before he leaves for Tokyo on Monday to attend the funeral of Emperor Hirohito?

"This is a very sensitive subject for Brazilians. You have to understand that any suggestion that we sell or lease the rainforest to foreign organizations is unacceptable."

We stress that the initiative for this project is Brazilian. It was Raoni's idea. We also stress that the foundation, whose members are Raoni, Megaron, J.P. and myself, will have its headquarters here in Brazil.

"That is why we want to work in partnership with you, we do not want to embarrass the government or work against you. We can raise millions of dollars and we need your blessing to use it properly. Can we have a meeting with the President?"

The noise outside is increasing. When we entered the apartment building, there were only a couple of children playing, now there seems to be a large crowd. The minister seems to have made a resolution. He gets up.

114

"I will call the President."

Jean-Pierre and I can hardly believe our ears. He leaves the room and his wife offers me another cold remedy. The crowd outside is definitely getting larger. There is a knock on the front door and, through the discreet opening, we see at least three news crews in the hall outside. Cameras flash, children scream and the door is quickly shut. I am now on my third bourbon. The phone rings, the President has called back. After three minutes, the minister returns, smiling.

"He will meet you at 11.30 in the morning at the palace."

So far, so good. We leave the besieged apartment in a flurry of autographs, flashes and abortive news interviews. We don't want to make a statement until we have spoken to the President.

"Let's go to the bar, J.P. I think we should celebrate."

IN THE PRESIDENTIAL PALACE

I sleep like a baby, and wake up without a cold. The only concession I can make to my presidential meeting is to shave. I didn't bring a change of clothes, all I have are my jungle fatigues.

The presidential palace was built in 1958 and is, as you might expect, modern and a little sterile, an abstraction of glass and steel amid hissing lawns and man-made lakes. J.P. and I look like a couple of tramps. The palace guards eye us suspiciously. The President is waiting for us. He is a handsome, rather dapper man with greying hair and a moustache. He welcomes us into his library, where we are seated at a large table. The French film crew are allowed to film the proceedings. The meeting is cordial and frank. As the President speaks I can't help but notice that his feet are nervously dancing beneath the table. What does this body language mean? It's a hard signal to read, but he speaks calmly and reassuringly of his concern for the environment and points out that under his presidency more land has been demarcated

for preservation than in any other period, that the jungle has to a large extent proved impervious to the schemes of man. J.P. is kicking me under the table. Indeed, there is more going on underneath the table than above it, between the dancing President and the impatient Belgian. J.P. and I get down to specifics: will he give us permission for the Park? After 45 minutes of discussion and looking at maps, the President agrees that, in principle, he will support our project. He has given us the green light. A round of photographs and handshakes cements our resolve.

Now for the Brazilian press who are waiting outside the palace gates. Someone thrusts today's newspaper in front of my face. The headline reads "Sting not coming to Brazil". Someone's in trouble. J.P. gets out his map of Brazil with a suggested border of the Park in red pen. I sign autographs, answer questions, and in between hum snatches of *Brazil*. I am very happy.

J.P. looks at his watch, it's getting late and we must arrive in the jungle before it gets dark. There are no landing lights, no computer-assisted touchdowns. We have to rely on the pilot's eyes and for that, we need daylight. We all have to cut our baggage down to under 10 kilos, and J.P. is worried because one of our pilots is a 250 lb giant. We need a smaller man or we might not be able to take off.

We have two twin-engined prop planes. Red Crow quietly blesses them with his sacred Indian pipe, and we're off. J.P. is unhappy as we were unable to find another pilot. The land below us is greener than it was the last time I made this journey. It's the end of the rainy season, in a couple of months there will only be red dust. We struggle upwards through the gathering cumulus.

After two hours, the riotous beauty of the jungle is below us, wild, unruly and mysterious, the dark womb of the earth. Then, the obscene sterile geometry of cleared land – Ying and Yang, masculine and feminine. Great rectangular swathes of unproductive rape. A few head of cattle graze among the dead stumps in clearings the size of Central Park.

We refuel at a cowboy town called Bang-Bang and buy some provisions. The storekeeper remembers us. Its a place I never thought I'd see again. The townspeople have already seen us on TV with the President. We only have half-an-hour to reach the next airfield and the outpost where Raoni is waiting for us.

The outpost, about ten wooden huts of corrugated iron roofs, was built ten years ago by white settlers on Indian land. When it was first built, Raoni and his warriors asked the settlers to leave, explaining that the land was theirs. But the white men laughed and offered the Indians hard liquor, knowing that Indians have no resistance to it. Raoni became very angry. The next day he returned with a war party and the white men ran for their lives, all the way back to Bang-Bang. The Indians inherited the outpost, but now it is infested with cockroaches.

OFF TO COLLECT RAONI

The plane lands again and Raoni is waiting for us at the end of the airfield with about a hundred Indians. I am very excited to be back here. Raoni greets us all warmly, especially Red Crow who he hasn't seen in three years. We tell Raoni about the meeting with the President and lay the map out for the elders. As the night draws in they all look very happy. We rig our hammocks in one of the huts and the Indians cook us a dinner of fish and rice. I'm too excited to sleep.

Up at dawn to wash in the river. Every square inch of the forest is animated, and the closer you look the more life there is. Everything moves, everything breathes. All of us are a little overwhelmed.

The morning is marked by incidents of forgetfulness and incompetence that can only be explained by our feeling that we are out of our depth. We are going to fly to Altamira, but first we need to refuel at Bang-Bang. There, we find we have forgotten the tripod for the camera, so one of the planes has to go back. Then we lose our money, $20,000 worth of cruzados that was locked in the plane last night. We turn the plane upside down, but not a sign. We have no alternative but to return to the outpost. Without money, we have no expedition.

J.P. goes to search the outpost. The Indians look bemused. I ask the film crew to search the plane again and once more the bags are strewn on the runway amid sisyphean grumblings. The bag with the money miraculously appears, to the amazement of the crew. I suppose it is a lesson about transcience and the instability of money: one minute it's there and the next minute it's gone, and sometimes it comes back. Let's leave now. The Indians think we are totally crazy.

Soon we are off again. Our plan is to take Raoni to Altamira, where a protest against a proposed dam project is taking place. Thousands of square miles will be flooded to provide electric power. The Indians do not want it. Their point of view is pretty straightforward.

The journey will take two days, flying over totally unexplored jungle where some of the Indians have never been contacted. We will spend the night with the Kayapo in a village on the margin of this vast, uncharted wilderness.

It's strange to see Raoni in the cockpit of our plane, proud in his chieftain's head-dress and body paint, surrounded by our technology, yet unfazed by it. The first time he saw his forest from a plane must have been wonderful for him, but with this gift comes the threat of destruction. From our height, we can see vast swathes of destruction, with cattle grazing on land claimed from the Indian forest land. There are farms already within the boundary of the park we are proposing. Raoni is agitated at their proximity and size. We ask the pilot for the co-ordinates of the farms so that Raoni can tell the authorities. We know that as soon as the rainy season is over the burning will begin again.

TRAVELLERS IN SPACE AND TIME

The village we are heading for has had very little contact with the outside world and promises to be our most authentic experience yet. We follow the river like the mysterious convoluted line of a dream. We are flying over another planet – a dreamscape of silver and green. To sight an Indian village from the air is to be left breathless, like travellers from another century. It looks like the idyllic village of Asterix, nestling by the shore of the river, surrounded by the wall of the forest. We land and turn off the engines. The silence stuns us and then we see the Indians, still and silent, watching us.

The tribe are a fearsome sight, their naked bodies painted black. The men have wooden plates in their mouths between their chins and their painfully stretched bottom lips. Their penises are tied up elaborately beneath straw cones. Some have ancient guns in their hands, others have clubs and spears. Raoni greets them first and reassures them that we are friends and mean no harm. The women have the tops of their heads shaved, with bizarre black face make-up. It is the meeting of two alien cultures. They are the fiercest people I have ever seen – proud and menacing.

I am happy to say at this point that the children are afraid of us, so we must look somewhat fierce to them, but the warriors display no such self-doubt. The chief arrives to greet us, an ancient with a head-dress of white eagle feathers that marks him from the rest of the tribe. Again, we get out the map, and Raoni explains what we hope to achieve with our Park.

The Indians have a way of looking at you which kind of opens you up. It would be hard to lie to these people. Some of the children are getting braver, they touch us and run away. I sit down in the grass and begin to write in my journal. I have a circle of children around me. The circle gets closer and closer as I become more and more absorbed in my writing. They are only a few feet away. From the corner of my eye I see them inch their way towards me. I suddenly yawn and they scream and run away.

I laugh, feeling like Gulliver in the land of Lilliput. Now the children laugh and get closer. I draw a smiling face in the book and hand it, with the pen, to the nearest child. He copies it, then I draw a glum face, he copies it, then I show him a trick with my hands, making my thumb separate magically from my hand. The children shriek with delight, I show one of them how it's done. Now we're getting somewhere. I

117

indicate for the children to take me to the river. They run through the long grass, naked and beautiful. This is truly the garden of Eden. One of the women is soaking manioc in the shallows and squeezing out the poison so it can be eaten. My new friends tumble into the river.

Raoni has the flu. He's worried about passing it on to this tribe. He does not want us to spend the night, but we don't have enough fuel to reach Altamira. We fly instead to Retenceo, a gold boomtown with a little hotel. We were on the front page of four newspapers this morning, also on the national TV news. They were very supportive. I think we have a real opportunity to convert the majority of Brazilians to our cause, as long as we can continue to be diplomatic and not aggravate reactionary and nationalistic elements in the government and the army.

I am very impressed by the lack of discrimination towards the Indians. We walk into a restaurant with Raoni and his warriors and he is greeted with great friendliness and respect. It is a good sign.

Altamira Blues

The next morning we fly on to Altamira. The journey is as rough as hell and we all have headaches from banging our heads on the roof of the plane. My knuckles are white from gripping my seat. Raoni is unafraid, he is looking at the pictures in the National Geographic. Below us the Xingu River is widening in its plain, preparing for its meeting with the Amazon.

At the airport Brazilian news crews, international news crews, cameramen, journalists and the army are waiting for us. It's a funny sight – myself, Raoni, Red Crow and J.P. guarded by a circle of soldiers who are all holding hands. We are chased through the streets of the town by the press and eventually lose our pursuers after a hair-rasing ride. We are staying in a private house, a safe house until the conference about the dams.

There are over a thousand Indians in Altamira and a local right-wing politican has threatened to bring in two thousand farm workers to confront them. Of course, if the farm workers don't turn up, they get the sack. That's why the army is in Altamira. There is a smell of violence in the air.

The Indian camp is about three miles outside the town. We follow the army patrol in a cloud of red dust. The town is desperately poor. If the dams come, then these people will have work. I feel sorry for them, driven from the cities by their poverty to live in the malarial fever of the jungle, hoping for a lucky break, a gold strike, a piece of land, who knows. There are many divergent points of view focused here in this little town and the poor whites have as much right to be heard as anyone else. Maybe the dam would help them, maybe not. But the land to be flooded would be Indian forest land, creating electricity that the Indians neither need nor want. However, dams are politically sexy, and the bigger the dam, the more important the politician.

I have never seen such an impressive collection of warriors, but if there are a thousand Indians, there must be at least as many journalists. Raoni is greeted by his nephew Paikan, the Kayapo's most eloquent spokesman, a man arrested last year for speaking out against the dams to the World Bank. Raoni looks the great chieftain that he is. He takes my hand, to protect me from the gathering throng.

We are led into a circle: on the one side, sombre and ferociously silent warrriors sitting in repose; on the other, an unruly and scurvy mob of media shouting and shoving, such poor ambassadors of our culture. The Indians are neither frightened nor amused, but are clever enough to know that in its chaotic and shambling way the media can help them, as long as they maintain their quiet, picturesque dignity.

Raoni makes a short speech and then calls on me to make an address.

I turn to J.P. "What the hell do I do now?"

J.P. smiles nervously, "You'd better speak".

"Thanks pal! It's nice to be here," I lie. "But I didn't come here to make a speech, I came to ask

questions. Are the dams the only alternative available to produce this power?" I suddenly catch sight of a government minister in the crowd, weighing my words carefully. "I wonder if enough research has been done on alternatives that wouldn't destroy the forest, because I believe that the Brazilian people want to preserve the rainforest as much as they need electrical power. I don't believe in the international-ization of the forest, it is Brazil's problem and Brazil must solve it, but the world community does have a duty to help Brazil in its struggle. I'm here today to launch an international campaign to raise funds for the demarcation of a Brazilian National Park, which would be the largest nature preservation area in the world. To protect the Indians is to protect the forest, and to protect the rainforest is to protect the ecology of the whole world. The Brazilian people know this, the President knows this, we want the world to know it."

I sit down, hopefully having demonstrated soli-darity with the Indians, sidestepped damning the dams, appeased Brazilian nationalism and promised foreign aid without threatening sovereignty. People seem generally satisfied apart from a few grumbles about the government. Am I becoming a politician? I check that my feet aren't tap dancing involuntarily.

"Not bad" says J.P. "Let's get out of here." We inch our way through a forest of cameras.

RANCHERS AND MINERS

We leave Altamira the next day and fly to a little town in the heart of Brazil's cattle country. The local farmers send a delegation to present their case to us. They don't want to be seen as the bad guys in all this. The deforestation is creating problems for them, too. We ask if we can visit one of the ranches. Can we bor-row a couple of horses, maybe we can ride around a ranch? The farmers snigger, but the manager of a nearby *fazandera* agrees that we can look around his ranch and ask a few questions.

When we get there the next morning we realise why the farmers were sniggering. The farm is the size of Los Angeles. It takes two-and-a-half-acres of land to feed one head of cattle. It takes much less land to feed a human being. The quality of the grassland decreases every year, necessitating more deforesta-tion. They clear the land with chains and bulldozers, leaving five mile strips of jungle between the areas of clear land. They do this because they know that with-out any trees at all, they will lose valuable rainfall. Also, the forest curtain acts as a windbreak and pro-vides a protection against disease.

They know the forest is their protector, yet they are forced to destroy it. Are they making any money? Not really. They are forced to freight tons of fertilizer north from Sao Paolo and the soil is simply quite poor. All the nutrients are in the trees, not in the soil. The ranchers are trapped in a cycle of destruction and more are added to their numbers every season.

"Who owns this farm?"

"An Italian consortium."

"Doesn't Volkswagen own one of them?"

"No, they sold up to a group of Japanese busi-nessmen, but business is not so good."

"How many workers on the farm?"

"About a hundred."

"How much are they paid?"

"A hundred dollars a month, which is above the national average. But the life here is hard among the flies and the intolerable heat."

We saddle up a couple of horses and take a look. Yesterday, we were Indians, today we are cowboys. We take a road in the shadow of the jungle wall, overlook-ing newly cleared land. The margin of the forest looks a little sorry for itself, but not as sorry as the field, where a family of eagles has made a home among the debris of dead wood. From the jungle, we hear a caco-phonous symphony of frogs. The sun is at an un-bearable angle above our heads. We kick the horses into a gallop so that the wind can cool our faces.

Soon we arrive at a farm worker's house, a con-crete block without doors to close or windows to shut.

121

Some ragged children are playing outside. Their bodies are covered in sores and bites around which flies play freely. There are no smiles, but a dead look in their eyes that contrasts so sadly with the joyful spontaneity of the jungle children. On the wall is the skin of an ocelot, shot while trying to steal a chicken. It must have been a beautiful animal. The farm manager offers us the skin. We say no thanks. He shrugs and hangs it back on the wall.

We say goodbye to the children, but they say nothing back. It's a hard life with few rewards, and these people have few choices in their lives. Twenty years ago, these farms must have seemed like a good idea, now no-one is so sure. The only people with a choice in the situation are the meat-eaters of North America and Europe.

That evening, we talk to a truckload of gold miners on their way to the goldfields. All they have are the clothes they stand up in. They will arrive in the goldfields with little money and no tools, which they have to hire from the company. The same is true of their food and lodging. So, from the first day they are in debt and only a huge gold strike will get them out of it.

They would be more likely to win the lottery. They extract the gold with mercury which pollutes the rivers, killing all the fish and eventually themselves. So here they are, packed uncomfortably in the back of a truck with another three days drive in front of them. They are one of the groups destroying the ecology of the Amazon, but when you see the desperation in their faces it is hard to be angry with them. They are driven from the poverty of the cities by an imperative will to survive, to strike it rich, but very few will.

A FAIRYTALE EXPERIENCE

The next day, we make our way to Raoni's village by boat down the Xingu. We have a 20-foot steel craft with two powerful outboard motors. I've been looking forward to a river trip since we got here. I sit in the bows under a bright red umbrella. Behind me are J.P. and Red Crow under a yellow umbrella. Behind them are the French crew and then Megaron and his wife and baby. Two Indians pilot the outboards and make good progress.

We are travelling with the flow of the river. The spray from the bow gives us our own rainbow arc across the water. We are riding a rainbow. The river in front of us is a glass ballroom of sky and clouds. The forest seems majestic. The great rivers of Europe and North America must have looked like this centuries ago. Once again, I feel like a time traveller. As the sun begins to sink, the sky turns to fire and everyone falls silent as our lengthening shadows race like dark gods across the surface. Storm clouds loom above us to impossible heights, red and angry, and in the drone of the engines I begin to sing.

In the last moments before darkness, we see a massive disturbance in the water on the far shore. As we get closer, our eyes straining, we see that all the children and young people of the village are in the river, leaping and diving in joyous celebration. There must be a hundred naked children in the chaos of the river. This is Raoni's village and all the children are painted intricately, some with the tops of their heads shaved, their faces made up in black paint. They are beautiful children.

We land the boat, the children escort us through the long grass to the village, and all around us are thousands of fireflies, giving the scene a magical quality. Some of the children have their hands around the tiny creatures. We are in the land of the fairies, and the children start to sing. This welcome is so beautiful, it is difficult not to cry. It brings up an emotion from somewhere very deep, our lost innocence, dreams of our childhood, a storybook perfection that is real, but so fragile that it has to be preserved.

A storm has now begun, the sky is a lightning grid and the thunder rolls around the sky in an endless circle. We rig our hammocks as the rain begins to fall. Too tired to eat, we fall asleep, the survivors of a drowned world adrift in our hut on the wild sea.

A FISHING TRIP

It is morning and the cock crows. We are no longer at sea. Excavating some toothpaste and a toothbrush from my bag, along with a few cockroaches, I head back to the river. A mother is washing her baby. To be connected to the river in such a primal way is ultimately to be responsible for it. It has long been my belief that the Indians here have a better understanding of existence than we do. They know where everything in their lives comes from, we don't. I don't even now where my shoes come from. People in the city may have a river running through it, but they have no direct contact with it. We pollute the river with impunity and shortsighted ignorance. How many rivers in the developed world would we dare to wash our children in? The Xingu is totally unpolluted from its head waters in the south to its meeting with the Amazon at Altamira. If the dams are built, then everything will change.

The Indians have offered to take us fishing this morning. It's a little late, but it sounds like fun. We set off down the river in our boat. The Indians have rifles, bows and arrows, and I ask Megaron what kind of fish we are looking for.

"Piranha."

"I was hoping you wouldn't say that."

"It's OK", he says, trying to reassure me. "It's probably too late for them anyway."

"You mean that they ate already?"

Megaron laughs and hands me some bait.

"Put this on the line and throw it out."

I think fishing is fine as long as you eat what you catch, otherwise it's just plain frivolous. But I don't want to meet piranha under any circumstances, prandial, sporting, or otherwise.

Megaron is churning up the water with his hand to mimic the sound of a fish in trouble. I can just see those razor-sharp teeth making a beeline for those tasty fingers and reducing them to skeletal strands within seconds. We wait . . . and we wait . . . and I have to say I've never been so glad to give up a project. The piranha have gone unmolested and so have we, although we have nothing to eat for tonight. It is now lunchtime, so we pull into the shore and seek the cool shade of the jungle. The Indians have prepared a little meat for us. It's tough, but we are very hungry.

"What are we eating?"

One of the warriors smiles.

"*Macaco.*"

"What's *macaco*, J.P.?"

"Monkey."

I stop chewing. Somehow, I'm not that hungry

123

anymore. Its time for dessert. We go into the forest to find some *caja*, a delicious fruit the size of a new potato, which lies in the undergrowth. It tastes a lot better than the monkey.

TRIBAL RITUALS

We arrive back at the village to watch a tribal dance performed by the warriors and the young women. The women are naked except for a sash of blue beads around their shoulders, the men in their feathered head-dresses hold their war clubs and rifles. It is a celebration of community, a ritual that bonds together young and old, male and female, in primal rhythms and melodies, handed down from generation to generation.

This continuity is vital to the survival of these people, a cultural bloodline that gives a sense of place and security to everyone in the tribe. The musical rituals in our own world often alienate young from old. The line of continuity is broken and maybe this partly explains our existential psychosis. We are lost in the chaos of an alienated society. This is why there is so much to learn from these people. They hold clues about who we are, how to live in harmony with our planet and not to destroy it. Perhaps I sound idealistic, but I think it's getting a little late to ignore the very clear warning signs that the earth is giving us.

The Indians think it is great fun to paint the white man in their ceremonial designs, but the problem is that the dye doesn't wear off inside a month. They won't take no for an answer, I will comply so long as I can design it myself. Black and white stripes will do fine, indulging my boyhood dream to wear the colours of Newcastle United.

The dance is over and the whole village heads for the river. This time I have to join in the fun. The river becomes a frenzy of splashing bodies and laughter, once again bonding the tribe to each other and to the river. The sun sets on another beautiful day, but anyone who spends the night in the jungle during the rainy season has to have a good reason. It may look like paradise during the day, but at night it is paradise for the insects. You sleep and they eat.

In a fitful slumber I dream that I am in a small airplane. The pilot is flying underneath powerlines, sideways down narrow streets. We can't seem to gain height. I wake up in a cold fever and the floor is crawling with cockroaches. The next morning we count the damage. I have a hundred bites on one leg alone. My back is pitted like the surface of the moon, and the face of one of the French crew is so disfigured with lumps that he looks like a leper. No one has escaped the night of the insects. I feel we have paid our dues to the jungle. We set off to inspect the landing strip, hoping that the heavy rain hasn't damaged it too badly. The children follow us. There are great puddles and muddy patches with occasional dry spots and the grass is very overgrown at one end of the strip.

It doesn't look too hopeful, and we need to be back in Brasilia today. Landing will be no problem, but taking off is risky, as the sticky mud might hinder our acceleration, landing us either in the river or in the jungle. The pilots will have to use their own judgement. We have an hour to wait.

As the morning mist clears, we are patiently sitting on our bags. We've already traded our hammocks, mosquito nets, flashlights and towels for bracelets, necklaces and a bow and arrow for my son. We look a bedraggled bunch of jungle derelicts in filthy mud-splattered clothes, hands and faces bitten to hell, hair matted into ludicrous stooge-like creations. I begin to laugh at Jean-Pierre. He returns the compliment. We are all laughing now. Whether or not the villagers get the joke, they are easily moved to laughter and then they are suddenly silent, turning their heads to the south. It is a few seconds before I realise that they have all heard the drone of the airplanes before we have. It is a disconcerting revelation. I turn to J.P. and he smiles.

"The jungle has given them more sensitive hearing, eyesight, a better sense of smell. In many ways, the need to survive here has made them into sensory supermen." I have to wonder how long I would survive in the forest alone, and this morning it is a low estimate.

Stormy Weather

Our planes warily circle the airfield. They make a number of passes and we are a little pessimistic, but in they come, bumping along the runway like toys. We take off and wave goodbye to Raoni's village. Their chief is still in Altamira. I just hope he makes it to Brasilia by Wednesday. I can't leave Brazil until Raoni has his passport in his hand. We are taking Megaron's wife and baby to Brasilia, the French film crew are going to stay a little while to do some aerial views of the village. They will join us later.

As we head south we see massive dark thunderclouds in front of us. There is no way around them. It's time to buckle up tight. Our tiny plane enters the massive wall of cumulus. Visibility is nil and the noise of the rain on the windscreen is deafening. We seem to be flying underwater. We are flung around this dark void like a child's plaything. Megaron's wife clutches her baby tightly to her breast, she is crying, terrified as we begin to lose our sense of direction. It feels as if the Amazon is a vast engine. The thunderclouds are its massive pistons, and we have somehow become trapped in one of the cylinders. I realize that the rainforest could destroy us at any moment. Our brave little plane struggles on, the propellers fighting for a steady purchase in the turbulence. The baby is screaming now, the pilot is sweating nervously as he fights to control the roller coaster. Our eyes are straining to see the forest below us. We must be out of this soon.

After an anxious eternity, the sun forces its way through the clouds, the forest reappears and the pilot releases a long sigh. I go back to writing, Megaron's wife and baby go to sleep. Red Crow is now 'White Crow'. J.P. has been smiling manically throughout the ordeal. Everything is calm and then comes the news on the radio that our second plane has crash-landed. After what we have just been through, the shock is almost too much.

The radio is now squawking unintelligibly, but we glean that no-one is hurt, although the plane is a write-off. We land in Brasilia without incident and learn to our relief that the crew is safe in Raoni's village. Another plane will pick them up tomorrow, but they're going to have to trade back their hammocks or they will have no place to sleep. I don't envy them another night like last night.

A Spanner in the Works

Back in Brasilia we receive an urgent telex from Bernard, in Paris, who is negotiating for Raoni to meet with President Mitterand and various European heads of state. One of the news agencies has picked up a totally bogus story about me fighting with the Indians. It's complete nonsense but according to a number of European newspapers I was chased out of Altamira by the Indians and had to be protected by the army. Bollocks. It seems that the old adage is true: a lie will have travelled round the world four times before the truth has even got out of bed.

The problem is that our international credibility has been reduced to zero and put our European tour in jeopardy. It is clear that we have enemies, but what is not clear is who they are. The story has already been discredited in Brazil, one journalist has been fired, another has resigned, but we really need Raoni here in Brasilia to demonstrate that we are working together and that there is no conflict.

There are a number of theories as to the source of the story. One theory is that it was the UDR, the right wing political party, another is that the hydro-electric company started the rumour to discredit opposition to the dams. It could even be a group of Indians jealous of Raoni. We must be careful not to allow The Rainforest Foundation to become a political football, but we urgently need Raoni, who is still in Altamira.

Unless he can denounce this bullshit to the world's press, all our plans will count for nothing.

We manage to get him on the phone. There is a FUNAI plane leaving Altamira today and Raoni could be in Brasilia tonight. All we can do is wait. We call back after two hours to make sure he is on the plane .. He isn't.

"Raoni, it's vital that you come to Brasilia, why didn't you get on the plane?"

He explains that three of his tribe are stuck in Altamira and as their chief his duty is to make sure that they get home safely before he can leave himself. We have no choice, we have to send a plane for him.

"Let's go out to dinner."

We drink a toast to Raoni arriving safely in Brasilia tomorrow morning and to our film crew trapped in the jungle for another night. "Damn the mosquitoes." "Damn the cockroaches." "Damn the press."

DELIBERATE HINDRANCE

Carlos, our production manager, is given the job of hiring a plane to bring Raoni back from Altamira. He hires a twin prop to make the five-hour journey there and the five-hour journey back. Like all of us, Carlos hasn't had very much sleep in the past week. He has to leave at two in the morning and at the last minute the plane is grounded for technical reasons. He asks for another plane. There isn't one – at least there isn't a prop, but there is a Lear jet.

J.P. and I are by now living it up at a disco in Brasilia, so Carlos bites the bullet and two hours later he is in Altamira and looking for Raoni. He's not at the hotel, so he goes to the FUNAI HQ. There are a few Indians there but Raoni isn't one of them. A FUNAI official assures Carlos that Raoni has already left. Poor Carlos is now in a panic, he has hired an extremely expensive Lear jet on his own initiative, to return to Brasilia without Raoni is unthinkable. He has to be in Altamira, but where? He makes his way back to the airport, maybe Raoni is waiting there . . . not a

sign. He looks back towards the town, the road is empty.

Carlos is in despair and contemplating suicide when he spots a FUNAI pick-up truck parked at a filling station. The filling station is not open yet so Carlos goes to investigate. In the back of the truck is Raoni, the most important Indian in South America, a chief of the Kayapo nation, asleep between two oil drums and shivering with malaria fever. Carlos asks him why he is here. He tells him that the FUNAI said there was only one plane coming and that would take him back to his village, not to Brasilia. The driver of the truck has now woken up. Carlos doesn't bother to ask any more questions, he grabs Raoni and heads off to the Lear jet. Raoni is very excited, he has never been in an airplane that flies so fast and so high.

A PASSPORT FOR RAONI

Two hours later, much to the relief of Carlos, they land in Brasilia. We meet them in the lobby, just in time for our meeting with the president of the FUNAI, who I'm sure isn't expecting Raoni. I'm happy Raoni is here, but he looks very fragile from attacks of malaria and the flu, which he can't seem to shake off.

As expected, the FUNAI president is more than a little surprised to see our celebrated Kayapo chieftain, but he manages a smile. There is an air of prosperity about FUNAI HQ that is not reflected in the field, where doctors and nurses have no medical supplies and haven't been paid for months. We are ushered into a boardroom with photographers, news crews and large, impressive maps of Brazil.

After the initial shock of seeing Raoni, the president recovers some of his composure. As President Sarnay has already given his approval to our project, our meeting today is merely a polite formality, but we don't want the FUNAI to be difficult, we still need Raoni's passport and this is their jurisdiction.

We outline the plan again, he nods, but tries to steer us away from demarcation. We reply that the

Foundation needs a project that will capture people's imagination. If we do that we can raise a lot of money, but we need the demarcation. He responds by showing us some pretty maps of the Amazon, telling us of all the plans to reserve land for the Indians. Raoni becomes very angry and emotional, he is having a malaria attack. He says all the FUNAI want to do is give his land away to the white man. His children and grandchildren will have nowhere to live.

The FUNAI president nervously tries to calm Raoni down and claims that in principle he agrees that our project is feasible, but a lot of research needs to be completed. Megaron tells him that research has already been done. The president sidesteps by telling us that Raoni can go to Europe with his blessing, the passport will be no problem after another round of photographs – there is definitely some political capital to be gleaned from pics with a pop star.

A couple of autographs, a slap on the back, a round of handshakes, a quick scrum with the secretaries and we're out of the building – now for the press conference. Jean-Pierre addresses the press first. A paper will later say he speaks the best Portuguese, which is probably true, but Raoni is wonderful – he speaks with great passion.

"Why do you journalists tell lies? Which of you is against our Foundation? Come on, tell me!" All the poor journalists try to become invisible.

"If any more journalists tell lies about us, I will chase after you with my war-club." The press sink yet further into their seats. Now this is the kind of press conference I like.

Well, whatever we set out to do on this trip, we seem to have achieved. We've made many friends, made a few enemies, certainly made the press. We have passports for Raoni and Megaron, agreements from the government as well as the FUNAI and, most importantly, I think we have the people of Brazil behind us. In the streets of Rio and Brasilia the reaction has been unanimous. Now it's up to the world.

That night, I fly north back to London. Below me in the darkness is the Amazon rainforest. I will be back.

127

THE RAINFOREST FOUNDATION

The Fundacao Mata Virgem, or Rainforest Foundation, was established early in 1989 to aid in the preservation of the Amazon rainforest and the indigenous people who live there. It grew out of the concern of Brazilian Indian tribal leaders and prominent Brazilian personalities over the devastating consequences of tropical deforestation both in the Amazon and around the world.

The goals of the Fundacao Mata Virgem are to

1) preserve areas of the Amazon rainforest surrounding the last remaining Indian tribes;
2) promote worldwide awareness regarding the Amazon rainforest and the indigenous tribes living there;
3) promote the inclusion of environmental studies in educational curricula throughout the world.

The address of the British branch of The Rainforest Foundation is

The Rainforest Foundation
5 Fitzroy Lodge
The Grove
Highgate
London N6 5JU